You Can Experience ...
A Spiritual Life

You Can Experience . . .

A Spiritual Life

by

James Emery White

WORD PUBLISHING

NASHVILLE

A Thomas Nelson Company

Unless otherwise noted, Scripture references are from the Holy Bible: New International Version®. Copyright © 1973, 1978, 1984 by International Bible Society. Used by permission of Zondervan Publishing House. All rights reserved.

Other Scripture references are from the following sources:

The Contemporary English Version (CEV). © 1991 by the American Bible Society. Used by permission.

The Living Bible (TLB), copyright © 1971 by Tyndale House Publishers, Wheaton, Illinois. Used by permission.

The Message (MSG), copyright ©1993. Used by permission of NavPress Publishing Group.

The Holy Bible, New Century Version (NCV), copyright © 1987, 1988, 1991 by Word Publishing. All rights reserved.

J. B. Phillips: The New Testament in Modern English, Revised Edition (PHILLIPS). Copyright © J. B. Phillips 1958, 1960, 1972. Used by permission of Macmillan Publishing Co., Inc.

The Good News Bible: The Bible in Today's English Version (TEV) © 1976 by the American Bible Society.

The Holy Bible, New Living Translation (NLT), Copyright © 1996. Used by permission of Tyndale House Publishers, Inc., Wheaton, Illinois. All rights reserved.

God's Word Bible (GW) © 1998 by World Bible Publishing.

Library of Congress Cataloging-in-Publication Data

White, James Emery, 1961–
    You can experience a spiritual life / by James Emery White.
        p. cm.
    Includes bibliographical references.
    ISBN 0-8499-3766-3
    1. Spiritual life—Christianity. I. Title.
BV4501.2.W4492 1999
248.4—dc21

99-37028
CIP

Printed in the United States of America
99 00 01 02 03 04 05 QPV 9 8 7 6 5 4 3 2 1

Contents

Acknowledgments

I am indebted, again, to my assistant, Ms. Devlin McNeil, as well as to the good folks of Mecklenburg Community Church. Graeme and Helen Paris opened up their hearts and home to me in New Zealand and provided me with daily afternoons in Eden Garden over Devonshire Tea, affording me the time and context for completing these chapters. And the greatest thanks to my wife, Susan, who once again made every page possible.

Are you tired? Worn out? Burned out on religion? Come to Me. Get away with Me, and you'll recover your life. I'll show you how to take a real rest. Walk with Me, and work with Me—watch how I do it. Learn the unforced rhythms of grace. I won't lay anything heavy or ill-fitting on you. Keep company with Me, and you'll learn to live freely and lightly.

—*Jesus*

Introduction

This is a book on developing yourself spiritually in light of the Christian faith. It is a sequel, of sorts, to *A Search for the Spiritual*, which was designed to help spiritual seekers explore and consider the Christian faith for their lives. This book is designed to help people who have chosen Christianity as their faith to develop themselves spiritually in light of that choice. This development is crucial, because the goal is not simply to discover a spiritual life, but to grow in it. That's what this book—the first in a series—will explore.

Developing yourself spiritually is not unlike developing yourself physically. If you want to develop your physical life, you invest in activities and pursuits that will develop your body. A developed spiritual life, too, will involve certain exercises. You will find these exercises, along with other activities, relationships, experiences, and investments, in each chapter. Yet there is an important distinction between spiritual development and other areas of self-improvement: If I work out to improve my physical life, I am *being* physical. If I engage in a book discussion group to develop my intellectual life, I am *being* intellectual. Not so with spiritual life: Spiritual exercises are *not* the same as *being* spiritual. By themselves, spiritual activities lead to nothing but lifeless religion. The heart of Christian spirituality is relational, not institutional, nor—a surprise to many—experiential. True Christian spirituality is intimacy with God, an ongoing transformation into the likeness of Christ.

Thomas Merton proclaimed that if you write for God, you will reach many men and bring them joy. If you write for men, you may make some money, give someone a little joy, and make a noise in the world for a little while. If you write only for yourself, you may read what you have written and, after ten minutes, you will be so disgusted that you will wish you were dead.

I have tried to write for God.

—James Emery White
Charlotte, North Carolina

CHAPTER ONE

The Search for the Spiritual

As part of a weekend retreat with a leadership team from my church, I participated in a team-building exercise on a ropes course. After some warmup exercises, our team was led to a field, where there was a several-hundred-foot climbing tower designed by someone who was later committed to a mental institution.

Okay, I made up the institution part.

But the designer should have been committed, because there was no sane way up this tower. The pinnacle could only be reached through a series of ropes, jumps, crossovers, and direct vertical lifts that seemed impossible from the ground.

Before the climb, I struck up a conversation with our instructor. I wanted to become acquainted with the person to whom I would be entrusting my life. Her name was Dee-Dee. She was a bright, articulate young graduate student from Arizona on leave to explore the field of experimental education. She had a quick wit, a ready smile, and an engaging personality. She was one of the most likable people you would ever want to meet.

After asking her a few questions about her background, she turned the tables and said, "So tell me about you guys. I know you're some kind of church group. What kind of a church are you?"

Still not knowing much about her, I tried to answer in a way that would enable the conversation to go in a number of directions. I said, "Well, we're a Christian church, but people attend from all kinds of denominational backgrounds—some have no background in church at all. In fact, we're kind of a church for the unchurched—for those who are open and interested in spiritual things but have been turned off to church in the past. Of course, people who have been Christians for years come as well and seem to really enjoy it."

Then I asked, "So what about you? Are you involved in a church or do you have any kind of church background?"

She responded, "Yeah, I go to a church now that I really like. It's kind of Christian, but I'm not sure. I was raised Episcopalian but got turned off to it pretty quick. And then I explored all kinds of things—a lot of Eastern stuff, even Wicca for a while, but that didn't do much for me. But I think I've found something that really works for me, at least for now. It's a form of Buddhist meditation."

"So," I asked, "is there a God for you in that meditation, or is it more of an internal thing?"

And she said, "Oh, there's a God—connecting is the whole point—but I'm not exactly sure who or what He is."

"It sounds like you're fairly serious about your spiritual life," I responded. "I really respect that."

"Thanks," she said.

"But what happens if this meditation thing doesn't work out for you? What then?"

"I don't know," she replied. "Keep searching, I guess; keep trying new things."

At that point, my heart filled with love for that young woman. She had a genuine desire to know and relate to God, yet her quest for spirituality left her still unsure of the destination. She was desperately searching for how to live a spiritual life.

By this time, it was my turn to face death on the tower. I went up and, by God's grace, came down. But I kept thinking about my conversation with Dee-Dee, and I wanted to have a final word with her before we left. Chances were that we would never see each other again, so I took a bit of a relational risk. As we were leaving the field, I pulled her aside and said, "Dee-Dee, I enjoyed talking with you earlier. If I were to send you a book to read, one for spiritual seekers, would you read it?"

And she said, "Sure, I'd read it. I'm always open."[1]

Aren't we all? We may not jump at every new idea or passing fad, but we are open to spiritual things. As Pulitzer Prize–winning historian Daniel J. Boorstin has observed, we are all spiritual seekers,[2] and today that spiritual search cuts across every generational line and demographic grouping.[3] Articles on angels, near-death experiences, prayer, and healing have become cover stories. The beginning of a new millennium has surfaced our strongest spiritual hopes and deepest spiritual longings. Spiritual themes run throughout contemporary music, from Alanis Morisette to

Madonna and from Jewel to James Taylor. A recent cover of *Swing*, a magazine that targets people in their twenties, ran a headline that captured the spirit of our age: "Spirituality Returns." People are interested in spiritual things, they're asking spiritual questions, and they are beginning to see that their deepest needs are spiritual in nature.

Even if we're not quite ready to say we long for spirituality, our desire for a greater meaning to our lives is inescapable. Mitch Albom spoke to this in his poignant collection of conversations with a dying mentor, *Tuesdays with Morrie*. Morrie Schwartz had been both professor and friend to Mitch. When he accidentally stumbled upon his former teacher's fight with cancer through a television program, Mitch reunited with Morrie and began meeting with him on Tuesdays to talk of life and death, purpose and meaning. Coming face to face with his dying instructor forced Mitch to take a closer look at his own life:

> *What happened to me?* I asked myself. Morrie's high, smoky voice took me back to my university years, when I thought rich people were evil, a shirt and tie were prison clothes, and life without freedom to get up and go—motor-cycle beneath you, breeze in your face, down the streets of Paris, into the mountains of Tibet—was not a good life at all. *What happened to me?* The eighties happened. The nineties happened. Death and sickness and getting fat and going bald happened. I traded lots of dreams for a bigger paycheck, and I never even realized I was doing it.[4]

Then Morrie addressed what happened to Mitch—or perhaps what *needed* to happen. As the relationship between Mitch and his dying mentor deepened, Morrie felt the freedom to tell Mitch that the things he had been spending so much time on, such as his work, may not have been so important. We often believe that if our outer world is cared for, it will translate into inner-world fulfillment. But the gulf between these worlds is wide. In the words of Frederick Buechner, we can use up our entire lives making money so that we can enjoy the lives we have entirely used up.[5] So how do we change? "You might have to make room for some more spiritual things," Morrie counseled Mitch. And then his old professor plunged in: "You hate that word, don't you? 'Spiritual.' You think it's touchy-feely stuff. . . . Mitch, even I don't know what 'spiritual development' really means. But I do know we're deficient in some way. We are too involved in materialistic things, and they don't satisfy us."[6]

He was right. Material things don't satisfy us. We want more, and we need more. And we know that this something "more" won't come from within ourselves, but from something outside of us that will transform our inner world. Douglas Coupland expresses it well: "Here's my secret: I tell it to you with an openness of heart that I doubt I shall ever achieve again, so I pray that you are in a quiet room as you hear these words. My secret is that I need God— that I am sick and can no longer make it alone. I need God to help me give, because I no longer seem to be capable of giving; to help me be kind, as I no longer seem capable of kindness; to help me love, as I seem beyond being able to love."[7]

But do we know what it means to find and experience the God whom we need?

COUNTERFEIT SPIRITUALITY

Few of us would consider ourselves easily deceived. We think that people *in general* can be deceived, just not us. This notion was put to the test by Scott Adams, creator of the *Dilbert* comic strip. He wanted to see just how savvy some hardheaded business executives were. So Adams, working with the head of Logitech International, the world's biggest manufacturer of computer mice, posed as a management consultant and held a seminar for company executives. Disguised in a wig and a fake moustache, Adams began by citing his credentials, which were—get this—working with Procter & Gamble's project to improve the taste of soap.

And nobody even blinked.

Then Adams led the group through an exercise that examined their mission statement. Their existing statement was "to provide Logitech with profitable growth and related new business areas." Adams told them that the statement was too simple. After getting them to brainstorm and share, he led them to produce a new mission statement for the company:

"To scout profitable growth opportunities in relationships, both internally and externally, in emerging, mission-inclusive markets, and explore new paradigms and then filter and communicate and evangelize the findings."

Hot terms, but pure gibberish. But they all signed off on it, as if this was a breakthrough! Adams didn't know what else to do to get these guys to realize what was being pulled on them, so the last thing he did was to draw a picture of Dilbert on the board. Then he took off his wig, took off his moustache, and announced, "You've all been had!"[8]

Rumor has it that they finally got it.

But if you had asked the executives on the front end if it was possible to be deceived like that, they would have said, "No way." But the truth is that we can all be deceived. We can be deceived financially. We can be deceived relationally. We can be deceived intellectually.

We can also be deceived *spiritually*.

And the great spiritual deception is that the *appearance* of spirituality is spirituality itself. I once heard of an Eastern holy man who covered himself with ashes as a sign of humility and regularly sat on a prominent street corner in his city. When tourists asked permission to take his picture, he would rearrange the ashes to give the best image of destitution and humility.

Was that true humility? Was that true spirituality? Of course not. But you'd be surprised how many people fall into that trap, not in crass, hypocritical ways—like rearranging their ashes to look closer to God—but in well-intentioned ways, confusing appearance with reality. And there are three main deceptions I will examine in this chapter.

The Deception of Morality

First, there is the deception of morality. It is easy to think that the nature of spiritual living has to do with being a good person or behaving in a certain way. This deception is along the lines of the

7

old cliché, "I won't drink, smoke, or chew or date girls who do." You look at yourself in the mirror and say, "God and I are okay. There are some very bad people in the world, folks like Hitler, but I'm not anywhere near being like them! So when it comes time for me to stand before God, I'll be okay. Compared to most people, I've lived a pretty good life."

I once heard a story of an army sergeant and a private who were doing survival training in the Rocky Mountains. As they made their way through the woods, they suddenly encountered a very large, hungry-looking grizzly bear coming toward them. The sergeant immediately sat down, ripped off his hiking boots, and took a pair of top-of-the-line running shoes out of his backpack. The private watched him and asked, "Sir, do you really think you're going to be able to outrun that bear?" The sergeant, sensing a teaching moment, put his arm around the boy's shoulder and said, "Well, you see, Private, I don't have to outrun the bear. I just have to outrun you!"

And that's how a lot of people feel about spiritual life. They think that spirituality consists of morality and that, in the final verdict, God will grade on a cosmic curve. Yet when we stand before God at judgment, we won't be compared to other people but to God Himself, who is the standard by which we will be measured. And none of us measure up to God.

If spirituality consisted of absolute morality, no one could hope to be spiritual. We are all immoral. I know I am. I have often identified with the confession of Joseph de Maistre, who said, "I do not know what the heart of a rascal may be; I know what is in the heart of an honest man; it is horrible."⁹ Romans 3:23 puts it bluntly: "All have sinned and fall short of the glory of God." Our moral lives will never warrant a relationship with God, much less support the spiritual life we all long for.

And that's not an easy truth to hear.

My friend Bill Hybels is the pastor of the largest church in North America, Willow Creek Community Church, just outside of Chicago. Early on in the life of the church, after Bill had given a talk on our sinfulness and our need for a Savior, a man came to his office and said, "All this talk about sin is making me feel really bad. I don't consider myself a sinner."

Bill felt he could shoot straight with this guy, so he said, "Well, maybe you're not. Let's talk about it. You've been married twenty-five years. Have you been absolutely one-hundred-percent faithful to your wife the whole time?"

He laughed and said, "Well, you know, I'm in sales. I travel a lot. . . ." They both knew what he was admitting.

"Okay," Bill said. "When you fill out your expense account, do you ever add something that wasn't strictly business?"

"Everybody does that," he replied.

"And when you are out there selling your product, do you ever exaggerate—like say it will do something it won't or promise to ship it tomorrow when you know it won't go out until next Tuesday?"

"That's the industry standard," he said.

Then Bill looked straight at him and said, "You have just told me that you are an adulterer, a cheater, and a liar. Repeat those words after me—*I am an adulterer, a cheater, and a liar.*"

9

The guy's eyes looked as if they were going to pop out of his head! He said, "Don't use those awful words! I only said there was a little something on the side, a little this and a little that. . . ."

"No," Bill said. "Just say it like it is. You're an adulterer, a cheater, and a liar. To me, that means you're a sinner in desperate need of a Savior."[10]

Just like the rest of us.

The Deception of Religion

A second deception is religious activity. The deception of religion is that when we go through certain religious rites, rituals, and memberships, or when we attend certain services or ceremonies, we are being spiritual.

This was what the religious leaders during Jesus' day believed. These religious experts were known as Pharisees, and they took the Old Testament and calculated that it contained 248 commandments and 365 prohibitions. And then they said that if you wanted to walk with God, you had to obey each one. And just to make sure that you didn't break one of those rules, they came up with rules about the rules and laws about the laws—more than *fifteen hundred additions!* So when the Bible said to rest on the Sabbath and not work, they figured up how many steps you could take on a Sabbath without it being considered work. They calculated that to take anything beyond fifty steps on the Sabbath was work and therefore violated the Sabbath law. So they would go through the day, meticulously counting how many steps they took. And they also determined that to make sure you didn't work on the Sabbath, you could eat, but not cook. And that you could bandage a wounded person, but not apply medicine. And to avoid committing adultery, they said you had to lower your head whenever you passed a woman so that you wouldn't even look at her. Soon the people who were considered the most spiritual of all were known as "bleeding Pharisees" because they were lowering their heads so much that they were always running into walls.[11]

It's tempting to reduce our inner world to such strategies, because our outer world is so subject to that way of thinking. We take a goal and break it down into policies and procedures. Think of the marketplace. UPS takes a lot of pride in the productivity of its work force. In fact, on average, a UPS driver delivers four hundred packages every working day. An article in the *Wall Street Journal* told how they do it: They micromanage every detail of that driver's routine, using three thousand industrial engineers to dictate every single task. A UPS driver must step from his truck with his right foot. He must fold his money faceup. He must carry his packages under his left arm. UPS even tells their drivers how fast to walk: three feet per second. They tell them how to hold their keys: with the teeth up using the third finger. And if a driver is considered slow, he is accompanied on his route by a supervisor who pushes him through the steps with a clipboard and stopwatch.[12] For the package delivery business, this kind of strategy works. But not in the spirituality business.

Because spirituality is not about religion, but a relationship.

Think of it like joining a health club. You want to look like Arnold Schwarzenegger. So you pay your money, go through the introductory class, and join the health club. You buy a T-shirt with the gym's logo, carry the card in your wallet, and proudly tell people you're a member. But that doesn't make you look like Arnold, does it? Of course not! A health club might be something you would want to invest in if you want to look like Arnold Schwarzenegger, but just joining, or even just showing up, doesn't do it for you.

Every religious rite, ritual, and ceremony is nothing more than an outward representation of something spiritual. It isn't the thing itself. Let's get very specific, because this matters. Have you been baptized—maybe as an infant—and you think that ritual established your spiritual life or gave you a relationship with God? Reflect carefully. Baptism is an outward sign of an inward change. Christ has asked everyone who has come to Him as Leader and Forgiver to be baptized. Baptism is one of the most important things you can do as a Christian. But it isn't what makes you a Christian. Though I do not come from a faith tradition that baptizes infants, those that do would agree, saying that this is what makes the process of confirmation so important. Yet many people have been baptized without it having any meaning for their lives at all. It was merely a rite of passage, like going through puberty or getting a driver's license. It wasn't a dynamic representation of their choice to enter into a life-changing relationship with Christ.

The same can be said of church attendance, taking communion, or being a member of a church. These are all good things, but again, they are reflections of someone's relationship with Christ;

they are not the relationship itself. This is why the Bible says, "For it is by grace you have been saved, through faith—and this not from yourselves, it is the gift of God—not by works" (Eph. 2:8–9). And the Bible also says that "people cannot do any work that will make them right with God" (Rom. 4:5 NCV).

The Deception of Knowledge

A third counterfeit is the pursuit of knowledge. This deception is the idea that all you have to do is to know and believe the right things. Head knowledge. Intellectual assent. Embracing Christianity on a philosophical level. But knowledge alone is meaningless. I can believe in a lot of things, but that doesn't mean these beliefs impact my life, much less reflect my life.

I spent about three weeks in the spring of 1994 at the Moscow Theological Institute as part of a teaching team that worked with Russian pastors who had never received any theological, biblical, or pastoral training. It was an interesting time to go to Russia. It had only been a few years since the fall of communism, under which Christianity had been outlawed and Christians had been routinely persecuted and imprisoned. Freedom was something new, something not wholly trusted to last. And many of my Christian students still bore the scars and serial-number tattoos from the gulags and prisons where they were imprisoned for their faith.

One of the churches I spoke at was a former underground house church that had worshiped together secretly for years under communist rule. Their faith was deep, infectious, and authentic. And it's no wonder. I once read of a similar house church that met in small groups at night throughout the week in order to avoid arousing the suspicion of the KGB informants. One of the underground small groups began to softly sing a hymn together, when suddenly two soldiers walked in, pointed their guns at the group, and announced, "If you wish to renounce your commitment to Jesus Christ, leave now!" And two or three of the members of the group quickly left, and after a few more seconds, two more.

Then one of the soldiers looked at the remaining group, pointed his rifle, and said, "This is your last chance. Either turn against your faith in Christ, or stay and suffer the consequences." And when he said that, he pulled the bolt back on his gun to make it ready for fire. Two more people slipped out into the night. No one else moved, including parents left with small children trembling by their side, each one expecting to be gunned down or imprisoned. Then one of the soldiers shut the door, looked back at those who stood against the wall, and said, "Keep your hands up—but this time in praise to God. We, too, are Christians. But we have learned that unless people are willing to die for their faith, they cannot be fully trusted."[13]

Whenever I think of that story, I am reminded that many people claim to believe in spirituality, but true belief is more than just saying that you accept the facts. Believing is giving your life over to what you say you believe. Believing is commitment. Take a look at how the Bible addresses this issue: "Does merely talking about faith indicate that a person really has it? . . . Do I hear you professing to believe in the one and only God, but then observe you complacently sitting back as if you had done something wonderful? That's just great. Demons do that, but what good does it do them? Use your heads!" (James 2:14, 19 MSG).

As Thomas Kelly once observed, the heart of spirituality has less to do with "knowledge about" than it does "acquaintance with."[14]

---

1. Material things don't last, and they don't satisfy us. How much more important are spiritual things?

2. Isn't it humbling to realize that nothing we ever do can make us seem good in God's eyes?

3. What are some rituals, or good works, that people do to try to be religious?

4. Why is true spirituality more about relationship than about religion? (See page 10.)

5. How does commitment reinforce belief? What examples of this have you seen in your life?

Chapter Two

Making a Change

One November, my family and I spent a few days in Williamsburg, Virginia, just before Thanksgiving. We stayed in a hotel that had a bathroom full of mirrors. Everywhere you turned in that bathroom, you were face to face with a mirror. At first, that didn't seem like that big of a deal—until the next morning, when I got ready to take my shower.

Susan had already taken her shower, so I jumped into the bathroom, got undressed, and started to step into the shower when suddenly I saw it—and it was ME! All of me! Everywhere I turned, I saw me from angles that I'd never experienced before and don't ever want to experience again. And it hit me in a way that it had never hit me before: I was fat!

Not pleasantly plump, not just husky nor big-boned, but FAT!

When I came out of the bathroom, my wife saw the look on my face and said, "Experienced the mirrors, huh?"

"Yep," I said.

"Well," she said, "me too."

So every morning for the next four days I had to face myself the way I really was. Prior to that time, I would have liked my weight to be different, but I hadn't really come to the point where I had decided for it to be different.

Until the mirrors.

Then I decided. Really decided. So I started a diet-and-exercise program that I've stuck to from then on—I lift weights, I run about twenty miles a week, and, during the last several years, I've lost more than seventy pounds, getting back—or at least close—to my basketball-playing physique. But the first step in that new beginning was the decision to change. It's not enough to know that you need to change or even to have the desire to change: You have to make up your mind that you are going to make a change.

Alfred Nobel, a Swedish chemist, made a fortune by inventing powerful explosives and licensing the formula to governments to make weapons. One day, Nobel's brother died, and a newspaper accidentally printed an obituary notice for Alfred. The obituary identified him as the inventor of dynamite, the man who made a fortune by enabling armies to achieve new levels of mass destruction. Nobel had the rare opportunity to read his own obituary before he had actually died and to see for what he would be remembered. He was shocked to discover that he would be remembered as someone who helped invent mass destruction.

So he decided to change.

He didn't just want things to be different or hope that things would be different; he determined that they would be different. He used his fortune to establish awards for accomplishments in various fields that would benefit humanity. And it worked, didn't it? If I asked you on the front end of that story what Alfred Nobel is best known for, you probably would have said the Nobel prize— the supreme award for achievement in the arts and sciences—not the invention of dynamite. But that would have never happened if he hadn't taken the first step and decided to change.

So how do you make a change and begin an authentically spiritual life? The simple answer is to become spiritually alive. This dynamic is captured in an intriguing conversation Jesus had with a man by the name of Nicodemus, who was a Pharisee. Their interaction, as recorded in the Bible, is well worth reading:

> Now there was a man of the Pharisees named Nicodemus, a member of the Jewish ruling council. He came to Jesus at night and said, "Rabbi, we know you are a teacher who has come from God. For no one could perform the miraculous signs you are doing if God were not with him."
>
> In reply Jesus declared, "I tell you the truth, no one can see the kingdom of God unless he is born again."
>
> "How can a man be born when he is old?" Nicodemus asked. "Surely he cannot enter a second time into his mother's womb to be born!"
>
> Jesus answered, "I tell you the truth, no one can enter the kingdom of God unless he is born of water and the Spirit. Flesh gives birth to flesh, but the Spirit gives birth to spirit. You should not be surprised at my saying, 'You must be born again.'"(John 3:1–7)

The search of Nicodemus is the search of many people in the world: a spiritual search for ultimate answers to life's questions. And like many people, Nicodemus is drawn to Jesus. Though he is not sure who Jesus is, he knows that Jesus is a man who comes from God, recognizing that God is in Jesus in a way distinct from other men. So he goes to Jesus—at night—because he's not quite ready to let just anybody know what's going on inside of him.

When Nicodemus gets there, he opens up the conversation by telling Jesus, "There's something about you that's different. You've got something in your life that I don't have in mine. I want to know what it is. I want to be in a relationship with God. Tell me how." Jesus looks him in the eye and realizes that he sincerely wants the answer—so He gives it to him. And it's one of the most fascinating, provocative replies that has ever been recorded. Take another look: "In reply Jesus declared, 'I tell you the truth, no one can see the kingdom of God unless he is born again'" (v. 3).

Jesus says, "You want to know the way? You must be born again." Nicodemus is more than just a bit confused. "The way is being born again? That makes no sense at all!" And we can understand his reaction, can't we? Our reaction would probably have less bewilderment and more cynicism. A modern-day Nicodemus would probably say, "You've got to be kidding me. I thought you were different. Born again? That's what the televangelists and radio preachers talk about—or scream about. That line is the butt of a hundred jokes. Please tell me you're not going to go that route."

But Jesus simply looked him in the eye and said: "I'm telling you the truth. Unless someone is born not only physically, but spiritually, he cannot enter the kingdom of God. Flesh gives birth to flesh, but the Holy Spirit gives birth to spirit. So you really shouldn't be so surprised that I would say you must be born again."

And that struck a chord with Nicodemus, because it spoke of something deeper than just *belonging*. Nicodemus was already a member of the Pharisees, the religious elite. And not only that, he was a member of the Jewish ruling council—seventy-one men who were the governing authority for Jews during the time of Jesus. And this wasn't about simply *behaving*. As a Pharisee, Nicodemus led a very moral life. And Nicodemus was so committed to the ritualistic purity of the Pharisees that he was made one of their leaders. And this wasn't about merely *believing* either. As a Pharisee, Nicodemus was devoted to the Scriptures. Jesus seemed to be calling Nicodemus to something deeper, something much more profound.

Jesus was talking to Nicodemus about a new beginning, a fresh start, and a chance to become a new person by entering into a life-changing, personal *relationship* with God. And once that became clear, you can only imagine Nicodemus's relief. He craved more as a spiritual being. He wanted a relationship, an encounter, an opportunity to come into contact with the living God and have his entire life reshaped, remade, reoriented—*reborn*.

THE NEW BIRTH

So how do you experience this new birth? The Bible points to four simple but very important steps.[1]

21

Admit That You Are a Sinner

The first step is to take a long, hard look in the mirror and own up to what God sees: someone who is precious to Him, but in rebellion. Admit that you have rejected His leadership and are, quite frankly, a sinner in need of a Savior. No rationalizations, no cop-outs, no excuses, and no qualifications. The first step toward becoming a Christian is total honesty and awareness of being a sinner before a holy God. The Bible says, "If we say that we have no sin, we are only fooling ourselves, and refusing to accept the truth" (1 John 1:8 TLB). The first step is to stop fooling yourself and to accept the truth.

Repent of Your Sins

The second step is that you must be willing to repent. The word *repent* isn't one that we enjoy hearing. It's a word that has been mocked, ridiculed, and even scorned, often because there have been some people who have used it in obnoxious ways. But *repent* is a good word because of what it represents: life change. When you repent of your sins, you're going beyond just admitting them—you turn from them. You realize that you have rebelled against a holy God, and you are sorry. You want to alter the course of your life in a direction away from your patterns of sinful behavior. This is why, in the Book of Acts, the Bible says, "Repent, then, and turn to God" (3:19).

Believe God's Message

The third step is to come with belief to the message that God has given in the Bible: Jesus was God in human form. God Himself became a man so that we would know what to think about when we think of God. As a man, Jesus lived the most perfect life ever known. He was kind, tender, gentle, patient, and sympathetic. He loved people. He worked miracles and taught people how to live lives that honored God. He was crucified and then rose from the dead, in order to take away the sin of the world and to become the Savior of all people. The whole Bible is built around the story of Jesus and His promise of eternal life to people like you and me. It was written for one purpose and one purpose only: that we would believe.[2] In fact, the Bible says, "If you confess with your mouth that Jesus is Lord and believe in your heart that God raised him from the dead, you will be saved" (Rom. 10:9 NLT).

Receive God's Gift

After you have admitted your sin, repented of it, and turned to God and the message of the Bible in belief, you then are ready to take the next step of receiving the gift of what Jesus did for you through His death on the cross. And what Jesus did on the cross really is a gift. The Bible says, "For the wages of sin is death, but the gift of God is eternal life in Christ Jesus our Lord" (Rom. 6:23). You should have died on the cross. I should have died on the cross. But God, in His love and mercy, chose to provide a way out. His gift is the forgiveness of our sins through the full payment of our sin penalty, which opens the door for us to be restored relationally with God. That's why in the Book of Ephesians, the Bible says, "Saving is all [God's] idea, and all his work. All we do is trust him enough to let him do it. It's God's gift from start to finish!" (2:8 MSG). But because forgiveness is a gift, it must be received. Like any gift, forgiveness can be offered, but it isn't yours until you reach out and take it.

To begin a spiritual life, you must deal with a single question: Will you admit, repent, believe, and then receive the gift of salvation and a relationship with God through Christ? Saying yes is just one prayer away, because the Bible says, "Everyone who calls on the name of the Lord will be saved" (Rom. 10:13).

If you want to take that first step toward authentic spirituality and become spiritually alive through Christ, here is how you can pray: First, begin by admitting to God that you are a sinner. Tell Him you know that you fall short of His standards, His holiness, and His character. Then tell Him that you want to be forgiven for those sins, that you want a clean slate, a new beginning, and an erased past. Next, tell Him that you want His leadership in your life, that you want to find out how He wants you to live, and that you want to live that way—under His direction. Finally, thank Him for doing it! Thank Him for forgiving you, for the leadership He is going to give your life, and for the relationship He is beginning with you.

If you pray that prayer and really mean it—if you come to Christ for forgiveness and a new life where He is your Leader—then you have become a Christian. Bells and sirens may not go off, but something miraculous and of eternal significance has taken place. Your life will never be the same. For a sense of how life-changing your salvation is, look at how the Bible talks about it: "When someone becomes a Christian he becomes a brand new person inside. He is not the same any more. A new life has begun!

24

All these new things are from God who brought us back to himself through what Christ Jesus did" (2 Cor. 5:17–18 TLB).

THE MYTHS OF THE SPIRITUAL LIFE

What can we expect from this new life?

Speedy Morris is the basketball coach for LaSalle. One day, he was shaving when his wife told him that *Sports Illustrated* was on the phone. He got so excited over the possibility of national recognition that he rushed through his shave and cut his face. Not wanting to keep the famous magazine on hold, he then ran out of the bathroom, which caused him to lose his balance and fall down the stairs. Limping, with blood streaming down his face, he finally got to the phone.

"Hello?" he said. "Is this *Sports Illustrated?*"

"Yes, it is," the cheery voice on the other end of the line said. "And for seventy-five cents an issue you can get a year's subscription!"[3]

Few things are as difficult to deal with as disappointment, and the heart of disappointment flows from our expectations. Nowhere is this more true than in our spiritual life, which is why exposing the myths of spirituality is so important.

The Instantaneous Myth

Comedian Yakov Smirnoff says that when he first came to the United States from Russia, he wasn't prepared for the incredible variety of instant products available in American grocery stores. He says, "On my first shopping trip, I saw powdered milk—you just add water, and you get milk. Then I saw powdered orange juice—you just add water, and you get orange juice. And then I saw baby powder—I thought to myself, *What a country!*"

The first misunderstanding about the nature of the spiritual life is that spirituality happens—instantly—at the moment you enter into a relationship with God. This false belief is that when you give your life to Christ, you experience an immediate, substantive, in-depth, miraculous change in your habits, attitudes, and character. Just add God, and presto! You get a spiritual life.

The truth is that entering into a relationship with God does nothing more than begin the ongoing development of that relationship. C. S. Lewis explored the intricacies of spiritual growth in his masterful work *The Screwtape Letters,* under the guise of correspondence between two demons over their "patient" on earth. Early on in the book, the human who had been the demon's subject of temptation becomes a Christian. The elder demon, named Screwtape, counsels his young nephew, Wormwood, not to despair, saying, "All the habits of the patient, both mental and bodily, are still in our favor."[4] The insight of Lewis's Screwtape is profound. Deep, lasting life change does not often happen at the moment your relationship with God begins. The Holy Spirit can do whatever He wishes, but even the most casual of observers would quickly note that He hasn't often desired to work instantaneous, miraculous life change in new believers' lives.

When you begin your relationship with God, your eternal destiny is altered, and you experience a radical reorientation of priorities, a new life purpose, and the power of God in your life. But rather than instant communion with God at the deepest of levels, you experience the beginning of a new relationship that will develop in intimacy over time. And rather than the immediate liberation from every bad habit or character flaw you've ever possessed, your experience is more like an army that lands on the beachhead and then begins routing out the enemy as it moves inland. This is why the Bible instructs Christians, "Let your roots grow down into him and draw up nourishment from him. See that you go on growing in the Lord, and become strong and vigorous in the truth you were taught" (Col. 2:7 TLB). Did you catch that language? You have to *let* your roots grow; you have to *draw up* nourishment; you have to *keep on* growing; you have to *become* strong and vigorous. Spirituality isn't something that just happens; it's something you have to be intentional about. Becoming a Christian is just the beginning of the journey; it's the start of a life that follows Christ. As Richard Foster has written, "Superficiality is the curse of our age. The doctrine of instant satisfaction is a primary spiritual problem. The desperate need today is not for a greater number of intelligent people, or gifted people, but for deep people."[5]

The Time Myth

Yet while Christianity is a journey, it is not simply a journey. Another myth is that true spirituality is merely a by-product of time. Becoming a Christian does not automatically translate into becoming Christlike. A five-year-old Christian will not necessarily have five years' worth of spiritual maturity.

I first picked up the game of golf when I was in graduate school. I took two lessons from a course pro, bought a set of clubs, and began to play. Initially, I made excellent progress. But then I began to play with less and less frequency. Soon, I only played at the annual Christmas gathering with my wife's family. As you might expect, I would play about the same each year—translation, horribly—because I hadn't played since the previous year. Recently, I have started to play with more regularity, and my game has improved dramatically. But if someone were to ask me how long I've played, the answer would be deceiving. I could tell them I've played for more than two decades, but that number of years is not significant, because I haven't been intentional about the game during that time. People who have only been playing the game a year but have consistently developed their game through lessons and practice could easily outplay me.

This is a crucial understanding. I can subscribe to golf magazines, purchase golf equipment, live by a golf course, wear golf clothing, watch golf on TV, and hang out at the clubhouse—and never improve my game! Simply being exposed to something has little bearing on whether we become proficient at it. While your spirituality takes time, it is not simply a by-product of time. The writer of the Book of Hebrews told a group of Christians that "though by this time you ought to be teachers, you need someone to teach you the elementary truths of God's word all over again" (5:12).

The Effort Myth

Another misconception is that spiritual growth is gained by trying. The idea is that people must simply decide to be spiritual, because spiritual living is essentially an act of the will. Love, joy, peace, patience, kindness, goodness, faithfulness, gentleness, and self-control are believed to be matters of effort. Yet while spiritual development demands intentionality, merely trying to experience life change can never bring about life change.

I can try very hard to bench-press three hundred pounds, but trying alone isn't what will enable me to do it. I will only be able to bench-press three hundred pounds by training to bench-press three hundred pounds. Michael Jordan was arguably the greatest basketball player to ever play in the history of the NBA. A whole generation of basketball players grew up wanting to be "just like Mike." They wanted to shoot like he did, jump like he did, jam like he did, and, most importantly, have their tongue hang out like he did. And they try! Hard! But few come close to mirroring Jordan's level of play. Why? You don't play like Jordan by trying; you play to his level by training. And not just any training but the training regimen he followed to play the way he played.[6]

The heart of Christian spirituality is to be like Jesus. And to be like Jesus you don't try either. You train. You do the things Jesus did in order to live like Jesus lived. That's why Jesus once said that "everyone who is fully trained will be like his teacher" (Luke 6:40). And the apostle Paul wrote, "Train yourself to be godly" (1 Tim. 4:7). "Anyone who is not a continual student of Jesus, and who nevertheless reads the great promises of the Bible as if they were for him or her," writes Dallas Willard, "is like someone trying to cash a check on another person's account."[7] The key to a spiritual life is to order your life around those activities, disciplines, and practices that were modeled by Christ in order to accomplish through training what you cannot do by trying.

The Solo Myth

A fourth myth is that a personal relationship with God through Christ is synonymous with a private relationship with God through Christ. The truth, however, is that becoming a truly spiritual person is a team sport.

If you have ever experienced or heard about Alcoholics Anonymous, you know that they have a startling record for life change. Lives that have been devastated and controlled by the abuse of alcohol have discovered radical transformation through AA's program. What is their secret? Many would say it is their "buddy" system. If you feel the urge to drink, you call someone who will support your effort to live the life you want to live. AA capitalizes on one of the great truths of true life change: Transformation is relational in nature.

This insight is taught throughout the Bible. In Proverbs, we read, "As iron sharpens iron, so one man sharpens another" (27:17). The writer of Hebrews said, "Let us consider how we may spur one another on toward love and good deeds. Let us not give up meeting together, as some are in the habit of doing, but let us encourage one another" (10:24–25). Throughout the Bible, you see strategic relationships in the lives of those who developed their faith with God. Jethro mentored his son-in-law, Moses. Moses then made a relational contribution to the life of his successor, Joshua. The prophet Elijah poured his life into Elisha.

Mary, the mother of Jesus, turned to her older cousin, Elizabeth. And Jesus set apart twelve men and invested His life into theirs.

The Transformation Myth

Yet these myths only seem to expose the ultimate myth—that to *become* spiritual, you have to first *be* spiritual. No! The Bible teaches that spiritual life comes before transformation. The transformation process begins when you come to God. The biblical order of events is to come as you are, receive God's gift of a personal relationship, and then enter into the transformation process.

And even then, it will often be a process of three steps forward, two steps back. This has been called the "law of undulation." To "undulate" means to move in waves, to go up and down in terms of your progress. And this is how human beings are when it comes to the flow of their spiritual lives. It is the nearest thing we have to normalcy![8]

The law of undulation is important to remember, because many people believe that true spirituality is gauged by feeling. Do I *feel* close to God? Do I *feel* spiritual? The reality is that authentic spirituality, while it is a dynamic enterprise that involves your entire being, has more to do with how you respond to your emotions than it does with your current emotional state. There will be times you feel up or down, high or low, but, in truth, your feelings may have very little to do with the actual state of where you are with God. The state of your spirituality does not rest on how you feel, but on who you are—and who you are becoming. God is in the soul-making business. He does

31

promise to transform you! You don't have to transform yourself or generate feelings of transformation. Take a look at what God said through the great prophet Ezekiel: "I will give you a new heart and put a new spirit in you; I will remove from you your heart of stone and give you a heart of flesh" (Ezek. 36:26).

FIRST STEPS

So how do you begin to change? If transformation is not instantaneous nor merely a product of time, how do you enter into training? Two ways: cooperation and investment. Let's begin with cooperation.

Cooperation

One of the ways I worked my way through graduate school was by coaching basketball. Some of the kids on my team had incredible talent and seemingly unlimited potential. I knew that if they would follow what I said, they could channel that talent into a team effort on the court and begin a path that could take them all the way to college competition—maybe even to the NBA. Here's what happened: Some kids cooperated with my coaching effort, and others didn't. At the end of the season, some of the most talented kids on the team were no different than when they started, while others had developed tremendously as athletes.

God, through the work of the Holy Spirit, wants to coach you. That's why the Bible says in 1 Thessalonians 5:19, "Do not hold back the work of the Holy Spirit" (NCV). And in Ephesians the

Bible says, "Let the [Holy] Spirit change your way of thinking and make you into a new person" (4:23–24 CEV). Circle the word *let!*

One of the wonders of the Christian life is that God actually takes up residence inside of you. He enters into your inner world, your moral conscience, and your spirit. That's why Scripture says in Galatians 5, "Let us follow the Holy Spirit's leading in every part of our lives" (v. 25 TLB). God wants to transform you. He wants you to come to Him as you are; to receive His gifts of grace, forgiveness, and love; and to let Him begin the process of molding you and developing you into all that you were created to be and do. He'll use everything from prayer to relationships, from the Bible to key events. But make no mistake—you will be coached.

But our metaphor breaks down if we make this process nothing more than coaching, because God will actually do a work of creation in your life. A spiritual life is something that God gives and develops through our relationship with Him. We must never reduce our spiritual life to something we develop on our own—it is the work of God in us.

Investment

This brings us to the second way we enter into training: investment. You have to take the coaching you will receive and the creative work God wants to perform and make the kind of investments necessary for that creative work to reach its maximum potential. Think of a mutual fund. You open the fund with an initial investment, say, one thousand dollars. If that is all you ever do, then the amount of growth in your mutual fund will be very minimal and very slow. You must make continued investments for the fund to move forward and begin to generate the kind of dividends and growth you desire.

Just like you can open a mutual fund but never invest in it, you can become a Christian and never become a disciple. You can begin a spiritual life and then never develop it. "Most of us turned to Christ when we realized there was a difference between Christianity as a religion and Christianity as a relationship," writes Ken Gire. "Sometime after entering into that relationship with Christ, we realized something else. That there is a difference between a personal relationship with Christ and an intimate one."[9] You must cooperate with God's leading and direction and make the necessary investments to position yourself for His ongoing work in your life. While spirituality consists of being, not doing, there are things to do that will help you be! And the goal of this book is to assist you in exploring those "doings" for the sake of your being, beginning with God's manual for spiritual living—the Bible.

---

1. What does it mean to be "born again"? (See page 21.)

2. With which myth of spirituality do you most identify?

3. What do you think it will take for you to grow spiritually?

4. Because it's so hard to develop spiritually alone, can you think of a person in your life who can help you grow?

5. Isn't it reassuring that when we cooperate with God's work in our lives and invest our time and effort, He will help us to grow spiritually?

CHAPTER THREE

God's Manual for Spiritual Living

Brilliant, learned, and handsome, Augustine held one of the most prestigious and enviable professorships in Italy. When he spoke, he was overwhelmingly persuasive. Few men considered themselves his equal. Although he had a Christian mother and was personally intrigued by the Christian faith, Augustine lived a life distant from God. He was torn about how best to live; he was engaged to be married, yet he had a mistress and an illegitimate child. In fact, he had many mistresses. Sex was necessary for him, he said, for he had no power to resist his natural desires. On the other hand, he was riddled with guilt from when he stole fruit from a neighbor's pear tree with gang of youthful rowdies.

But change was afoot in Augustine's heart. The great philosophers, such as Plato, had convinced Augustine that there was more to the world than what could be seen, tasted, touched, heard, or smelled. Augustine was coming to believe that things could be real beyond his own sense of reality. Then came Ambrose, a Christian pastor in Milan whose preaching Augustine was eager to hear. In Ambrose, Augustine found a speaker equal to his own oratorical skills. But Augustine soon became interested in more than Ambrose's verbal skill—he was intrigued with what Ambrose was *saying*. Augustine had tried reading the Scriptures as a teenager, but he was not impressed. At the time, he had been in love with beautiful language, and the language of Scripture had seemed dull and plain. But years had passed since then. Under Ambrose's influence, the simplicity of Scripture began to sound like the simplicity of the *profound*.

One evening, Augustine sat in his garden, utterly silent in the stillness of the summer heat. But inside his heart, a storm was raging. Confusion over his life built up until finally it seemed as if his chest would burst. He threw himself under a fig tree, sobbing, unable to stop.

Then . . . he heard a voice.

The childish, piping voice was so high-pitched that he could not tell whether it was male or female. The voice seemed to come from a nearby house. The child chanted, over and over, "Take up and read. Take up and read. Take up and read."

Were the words for him?

"Read what?" Augustine shouted into the sky.

Then he glanced around him, and there, lying nearby, were the letters of the apostle Paul from the New Testament. Was he to take up the Scriptures and read?

He snatched up the Scripture and began reading where it fell open—Romans 13. The words of verses 13 and 14 burned into his mind: "Let us behave decently, as in the daytime, not in orgies and drunkenness, not in sexual immorality and debauchery, not in dissension and jealousy. Rather, clothe yourselves with the Lord Jesus Christ, and do not think about how to gratify the desires of the sinful nature." Instantly, the shadows of his heart fled before the streams of light. The same Scriptures he once dismissed as a mere fable lacking in clarity and grace of expression altered the entire trajectory of his life and gave him what he had sought for so long: He had finally encountered *truth*.

Augustine gave his life to Christ. And for the next forty-four years, Augustine continued to "take up and read," becoming one of the most influential Christian thinkers and writers in history. But it all started in the garden, where he learned that the Scriptures were not just words to be interpreted; they were words that interpreted the *reader*.[1]

A VERY SPECIAL BOOK

The Bible, because of its enormous value to spirituality, is civilization's best-selling and most influential book. The Bible is a collection of sixty-six writings penned by more than forty authors during a period of several hundred years. To date, it has been translated into at least twelve hundred languages, and between thirty and fifty million Bibles are sold each year.

But why is the Bible so favored as a spiritual text? Simply put, it is inspired by God Himself.[2] Sometimes we use the word *inspired* to mean that something was wonderfully creative, such as a painting by

Michelangelo or a concerto by Handel. Sometimes we use the word *inspired* to refer to how something impacts us, such as a dramatic speech or a touching act. Inspiration, as it relates to the Bible, is much more profound. The apostle Paul declared, "All Scripture is God-breathed" (2 Tim. 3:16). "God-breathed" means that the writing is from God Himself! More than three thousand times in the Bible we find the writers using some form of the expression "The Lord says," referring to their belief that they were conveying the very Word of God. For example, the Bible records God saying to the prophet Jeremiah: "I have put my words in your mouth" (Jer. 1:9). The idea of inspiration is that God used people to write the books of the Bible, but He was so involved in the process that they wrote exactly what He wanted. One of the clearest expressions of this idea is found in the Book of 2 Peter: "Above all, you must understand that no prophecy of Scripture came about by the prophet's own interpretation. For prophecy never had its origin in the will of man, but men spoke from God as they were carried along by the Holy Spirit" (1:20–21).

The Bible does not suggest that it is merely a collection of human opinion, but something that is foundationally true and trustworthy, literally God's Word to us. As the apostle Paul explained in 2 Timothy: "The whole Bible was given to us by inspiration from God and is useful to teach us what is true and to make us realize what is wrong in our lives; it straightens us out and helps us do what is right. It is God's way of making us well prepared at every point" (3:16–17 TLB).

This is why the word *revelation* is often used to describe the Bible, coming from the Latin word *revelatio,* which means to "draw back the curtain." The Bible is God revealing Himself and truth about Himself that could not otherwise be known. But that's not all—it's also God revealing truth about *us* we could not otherwise know. The Bible gives guidance and direction for virtually every area of life, including work, marriage, family, relationships, finances, emotions, and even physical health. The comprehensive nature of the Bible is significant, because we tend to think of our spiritual life as just one aspect of living, instead of life itself. There is no such thing as a spiritual life—there's just life. And for life to be spiritual, God must envelop every dimension of it. But how do you take the Bible and allow it to affect your life in such a complete way?

A few years ago, on Father's Day, I received my typical assortment of unusual gifts. With four young children, *unusual* is usually an understatement. Like many dads, I got some ties, only mine had the distinction of being handmade. And they weren't neckties; they were handmade *bow* ties. I got lots of cards, a special Father's Day book, and a bunch of hugs, kisses, and neck rubs. But in all of that was a present from my then six-year-old daughter, Rachel. She had worked on it tirelessly, and she wouldn't let anyone see it or know what it was. Finally, on Father's Day, she brought it out. Her grand creation was a box, covered in white paper, with a big hole cut out of it. On the top, she had glued two plastic glasses.

I looked at it and did what any good father would have done. I told her it was *beautiful,* thanked her over and over, and gave her a great big hug and a kiss. Then when she left the room, I turned to my wife and said, "Now what exactly *is* this?"

She said, "Honey, I don't have any idea."

"Well, what am I supposed to do with it?"

She said, "I don't know, but you'd better find some way to use it, or you're going to have one sad little girl on your hands."

So I decided to go to the source. I went downstairs, found Rachel, and said, "Honey, I forgot something very important. I was so impressed by how hard you worked and how pretty this was that I forgot to ask you what you would most like me to *do* with it, because there are so many things it would be good for."

Not bad, huh? But then she looked at me and said, "Daddy, don't you know?"

I said, "Well, sure, kind of, but there's just so *many* things I could do with it—and I wanted *you* to tell me what you *most* wanted me to do with it."

She said, "I want you to use it the way everybody does!"

This wasn't going well at all. Fortunately, my oldest daughter jumped in and saved me. She said, "Rachel, what *is* that thing, anyway?" Exasperated, Rachel rolled her eyes and said, "It's a bookcase with a bull's head on it!" Don't laugh—I've had to live with that bull's head for many years.

Have you ever felt that way about the Bible? There's no doubt in your mind that the Bible is special, but you're not quite sure what to do with it? Don't worry, you're not alone. Here are three steps that will help you take the Bible and have it operate in your life.

Read It

The first step is to read what the Bible says. Jesus was once asked a number of questions by a group of spiritual seekers. He answered them patiently, but finally, after a number of questions, He said something intriguing: "You do not know the Scriptures. . . . Have you not read what God said to you?" (Matt. 22:29, 31). Jesus was surprised that people who claimed to be interested in spiritual things had never bothered to read the main text.

Get a Modern Translation

So how do you read the Bible? First, I would suggest that you get hold of a modern translation or paraphrase of the Bible. Many people who have tried to read the Bible before have found it difficult reading, and for good reason—it was! Most of the time, this difficulty has less to do with the text itself than it does with the *translation*. The Bible was written, basically, in two languages: Hebrew and Greek. The Old Testament was written in the language of its day—Hebrew—and the New Testament was written in the language of its writers—Greek. That means that all of our Bibles today are translations of those original languages. For instance, when the Bible was translated in the seventeenth century, the Greek and Hebrew manuscripts were translated into the language of that day, which meant that there were a lot of "thees" and "thous." Since it was commissioned by King James, it was called the King James Version. But there's nothing magical or holy about King James English, and we don't use King James English today. So get a modern translation that takes the manuscripts of the Bible and translates them into the language of our day, which will make it much easier for you to read and understand what it says.[3]

41

Start with the Gospels

A second suggestion for reading the Bible is to remember that it is a library of writings, which means you have freedom as to where you begin reading. In fact, when it comes to the Bible, it is probably *not* best to start on page one in the first book—Genesis—and then work your way through to the end of the last book—Revelation. Most seasoned readers of the Bible would suggest you start off with one of the four biographies of the life of Jesus, which would be the New Testament Gospels of Matthew, Mark, Luke, and John (named after the men who wrote them). Matthew was written to the Jews of his day. Mark was the youngest of the four biographers, and his Gospel is the shortest and filled with the most action scenes. Luke was the scholar of the group and is commonly ranked as a first-class historian in light of his eye for detail. John was the philosopher of the group and occasionally wrote of the life of Jesus in light of certain categories within Greek philosophical thought. So begin by choosing one of these four, and jump in. Whichever one you choose will give you a good foundation of the central message of the Bible, which is Jesus and His life and teaching. After that, go to another New Testament book, like James, which is a brief letter to some of the early church communities that will give you a taste of the Bible's practical advice on patterning your life after Christ. Then go back and read Genesis to get a feel for some of the main characters of the Bible and how God interacted with their lives. After you read those three books, you're probably in good shape to jump in wherever you want.

Take Heart

A third suggestion is to begin reading the Bible with a positive, "can-do" attitude. Don't be intimidated! If you begin reading the Bible with the idea that you probably won't be able to understand it, you'll be much more likely to put it down at the first rough spot. The truth is that it's not that hard to understand what you'll be reading. The Bible was written by ordinary folks to other ordinary folks. In fact, one of the primary writers of the New Testament, the apostle Paul, once said, "We do not write you anything you cannot read or understand" (2 Cor. 1:13). So take heart! If you get a good, up-to-date translation and start off in the right place, you will find the Bible to be a pretty good read.

Discover

Fourth, read the Bible with an eye toward discovery. Think of the kind of questions an investigative reporter arriving on the scene of a breaking story would ask: "Who? What? Where? When? Why? How?" This is the work of observation. So when you read the Bible, ask questions like, "Who is speaking? To whom was this passage written? What are the main ideas?"

Once you've asked the basic questions, you can go even deeper, probing beyond what the text itself offers on the surface. "What was the background of the writer? What was the background of the recipient? What seems to be the key section or verse?" Once you've done this, you can move on to interpretation, which is analyzing what it *means.* The heart of this is to find out what the passage *originally* meant and then progress to the principle behind the meaning.

43

Read with a Heart of Reflection

Finally, along with an eye toward discovery, you should read the Bible with a heart for reflection. The Hebrew word for *meditate* means "to mutter or to mumble, to make a low sound." It was the habit of people reflecting on the Scriptures to turn the words and meanings over and over in their minds, and they did this by repeating the words to themselves, often in a whisper that sounded very much like mumblings. The point is not to verbally repeat the words you study aloud, but to so reflect upon them that they penetrate into the depths of our hearts.[4]

There is a story of a very learned man who came to visit a rabbi. The scholar was no longer a young man—he was close to thirty—but he had never before visited a rabbi.

"What have you done all your life?" the rabbi asked him.

"I have gone through the whole of the Talmud three times," answered the learned man.

"Yes, but how much of the Talmud has gone through you?" the rabbi inquired.[5]

Believe It

But reading the Bible is only the first step. The second step is to *believe* what we read. When it says that a certain action is best, a particular idea is true, or a specific event took place, you must make the choice to believe it, else its power and significance will be lost on your life.

Now, whether to believe the Bible is an issue for anyone who is exploring the Christian faith.[6] But once the line of faith has been crossed, its pages come alive as the very Word of God to us on the ultimate questions and issues of life. The Bible doesn't claim to be merely a collection of human opinion; it claims to be God's inspired and written Word to us, and as a result, something to believe in. You cannot play the role of senior editor and cut out what you don't like or choose to embrace in the Bible. True belief is when you no longer set yourself up as the judge of the Bible but instead let the Bible be the judge of you.

Follow It

After you read the Bible and make the choice to believe it by faith, you must take the important step of *following* it. The wisdom Solomon captured in the Proverbs says, "Despise God's Word and find yourself in trouble. Obey it and succeed" (13:13 TLB). Reading and believing should lead to *doing*. If you don't move to this final step, then you've missed one of the primary roles of the Bible for your life. This final step is so important that I want to explore the different ways we can shortchange the Bible's impact on our spiritual lives by failing to do what it says.

The Cosmic Exception Clause

Most of us are familiar with exception clauses: Something applies to most people and most situations, except when . . . and then the exceptions are noted. Sometimes exceptions are important, helping us to avoid the bureaucracy that can come with a one-dimensional approach. But many times the idea that there are exceptions can be dangerous and can lead to great harm. When a sign says, "Warning:

Electrified Fence—Do Not Touch," the idea of an exception does not apply. The Bible is like that. It is a comprehensive manual for doing life and relating to God. You cannot read the Bible with the attitude that allows you to say, "In my case and in my situation, I've been given a cosmic exception clause from the Word of God," whenever you come to something you do not like or agree with. That's not following God, and that attitude will never allow you to grow in your spirituality. The Bible says, "The man who says, 'I know him,' but does not do what he commands is a liar, and the truth is not in him. But if anyone obeys his word, God's love is truly made complete in him. This is how we know we are in him: Whoever claims to live in him must walk as Jesus did" (1 John 2:4–6).

The Cafeteria Line

A second pitfall to avoid when it comes to following the Bible is a "cafeteria-line" approach. You grab your tray and start down the line. Some things you like, and some things you don't. So what will end up on your plate—things you hate? I don't think so. Your natural instincts will be to pile your plate with food that catches your eye and that you think will taste good.

Now think of a cafeteria-line approach to the Bible. You go down the food bar of biblical truth, pick out what you like, and put it on your tray. If you see something that you don't like, you just don't put it on your plate. So you end up with some comfortable insights and principles on things like marriage or parenting but pass up the uncomfortable, lifestyle-changing applications on money or sex. Why go for spinach when there's cheesecake? So at the end, you walk away with only the areas of God's leadership in your life that you like. The ones that go down easy. The ones that taste good. But because you have food on your plate, you say, "See, I'm letting God lead my life." But you're not. When you approach the Bible like a cafeteria line, you're the one in charge. All you've done is assign God a place in your back pocket where you can whip Him out whenever He's comfortable and put Him away whenever He's not. A willingness to follow whatever the Bible says is such a litmus test of authentic spirituality that Jesus declared: "Not all who sound religious are really godly people. They may refer to me as 'Lord,' but still won't get to heaven. For the decisive question is whether they obey my Father in heaven. At the Judgment many will tell me, 'Lord, Lord, . . .' But I will reply 'You have never been mine'" (Matt. 7:21–23 TLB).

The Great Compromise

A third way to make the Bible impotent in your life is to engage in the great compromise. To compromise something is to weaken it, lower it, and strip it of its power and potency. How do you compromise the Bible? First, by watering down its clear *teaching,* and second, by watering down its clear *authority.*

Let's say you come across a certain area where God clearly calls you to follow Him. But you don't want to follow Him in that area. You don't want to come right out and *admit* that, so you say, "I don't think the Bible is very clear in that area"—a compromise of the Bible's teaching—or "I want to follow God, but I'm not sure the Bible's right on this at all"—a compromise of biblical authority.

My friend Lee Strobel talks about this in the following way: Pretend that your daughter and her boyfriend are going out for a Coke on a school night. You say to her, "You must be home before eleven." Now suppose it gets to be 10:45, and the two of them are still having a great time. They don't want the evening to end, so suddenly they begin to have difficulty interpreting your instructions. They say, "What did he really mean when he said, '*You* must be home before eleven?' Did he literally mean us, or was he talking about *you* in a general sense, like people in general? Was he saying, in effect, 'As general rule, people must be home before eleven?' Or was he just making the observation that 'Generally, people are in their homes before eleven?' I mean, he wasn't very clear, was he?

"And what did he mean by, 'You *must* be home before eleven?' Would a loving father be so adamant and inflexible? He probably means it as a suggestion. I know he loves me, so isn't it implicit that he wants me to have a good time? And if I am having fun, then he wouldn't want me to end the evening so soon.

"And what did he mean by, 'You must be *home* before eleven?' He didn't specify *whose* home. It could be anybody's home. Maybe he meant it figuratively. Remember the old saying, 'Home is where the heart is?' My heart is right here, out having a Coke, so doesn't that mean I'm already home?

"And what did he really mean when he said, 'You must be home before *eleven?*' Did he mean that in an exact, literal sense? Besides, he never specified eleven P.M or eleven A.M. And he wasn't really clear on whether he was talking about Central Standard Time or

Eastern Standard Time. I mean, it's still only quarter to seven in Honolulu. And as a matter of fact, when you think about it, it's *always* before eleven. Whatever time it is, it's always before the next eleven. So with all of these ambiguities, we can't really be sure what he meant at all. If he can't make himself more clear, we certainly can't be held responsible."[7]

There's no doubt that some parts of the Bible are hard to understand. It reflects the places, histories, cultures, and languages of people long ago and far away. Sometimes you have to have some background information on those issues to know how best to apply it to your life. And there are some passages about which people might disagree. But on the essential teachings and issues, the Bible leaves little room for confusion. As Mark Twain was known to quip, "It's not the parts of the Bible I don't understand that disturb me, rather it's the parts of the Bible that I do understand that disturb me."

There's a reason we feel this way. Truth is not comfortable, and neither is the life change it brings when it is applied. We often want to run away, escape, and get out from underneath its weight. As the Bible says, "For whatever God says to us is full of living power; it is sharper than the sharpest dagger, cutting swift and deep into our innermost thoughts and desires with all their parts, exposing us for what we really are" (Heb. 4:12 TLB). But isn't that what we all want? Don't we want our lives addressed at the deepest levels and then transformed and energized from the inside out? One of the great ironies of spiritual development is our constant temptation to flee every step of the way from the very thing that will give us what we most desire. This is why applying the Bible to your life is so crucial, asking yourself questions like:

- What attitude do I need to change?

- What do I need to start doing—or stop doing?

- What things do I need to stop believing—or start believing?

- What relationships do I need to reconcile?

- What ministry should I be having with others?[8]

Our goal is to become like soft clay in the hands of a master potter, letting God shape us as He desires. Following Christ is a relational issue, not some dead, lifeless embrace of a set of dos and don'ts. It's a reflection of a love relationship. It's not an "ought to" as much as a "want to." It's not duty as much as devotion. That is why Jesus said, "If anyone loves me, he will obey my teaching. . . . He who does not love me will not obey my teaching" (John 14:23–24).

Obedience matters. Shot down over Bosnia in 1995, Captain Scott O'Grady spent six days living off of bugs and rainwater before he was rescued by a daring band of young marines. The affair brought a great deal of attention to O'Grady, but it also turned the eyes of the world to the seventeen-day survival course he had taken at Fairchild Air Force Base near Spokane, Washington, that was instrumental in his ability to sustain his life. There he was taught how to live off of the land, what to eat and what not to eat, how to gather water, and how to stay warm at night. O'Grady would be the first to tell you that just *knowing* the information, and even believing in it, were not enough. Once he was shot down, he had to *apply* what he had learned, and it was the application to his life that made the difference. Consider the Bible your "survival-course" manual. Read it, know what it says, believe it, and—most importantly—apply it.

---

1. What's significant about the fact that the Bible was inspired by God and not just written by human beings?

2. The Bible is a timeless book, in that God covered even the topics that are important to us today, like work, marriage, family, relationships, finances, stress, love, health, and time. Which areas of life are you most thankful that God's Word covers?

3. It's so easy to divide life into separate categories (work, family, exercise, spirituality, etc.). Why is it important not to just keep spirituality in a separate box off to the side?

4. After we read the Bible, it's important to believe it and follow it. Why is that often difficult?

CHAPTER FOUR

Talking to God

A poll by the Gallup Organization found that nine out of every ten American adults say they pray.[1] They pray for their families, for world peace, for safety, for strength to meet the challenges of life, and for guidance with important decisions. One out of every four people pray for their favorite sports team to win a game! And Gallup found that we don't just pray every now and then. Most people who pray do so once or even twice a day.[2] So what is it we're all doing? How are we supposed to do it? What happens when we do it? Let's begin with prayer itself.

WHAT IS PRAYER?

According to the Bible, prayer is three things: communication, conversation, and communion with God.[3]

Prayer Is Communication

First, prayer is communication with God. It is the vehicle by which we, as human beings, talk to God. It's how we tell Him what we want Him to know and what we'd like Him to do.

The Bible tells the story of a man named David who was a great king over Israel. He understood how to communicate with God, and, as a result, his life is an excellent model for prayer.

Sometimes David prayed for help: "Listen to my cry for help, my King and my God, because I pray to you" (Ps. 5:2 NCV).

Sometimes David prayed for forgiveness: "There was a time when I wouldn't admit what a sinner I was. But my dishonesty made me miserable and filled my days with frustration . . . until I finally admitted all my sins to you and stopped trying to hide them. I said to myself, 'I will confess them to the Lord.' And you forgave me! All my guilt is gone" (Ps. 32:3, 5 TLB).

Sometimes all David wanted to do was to honor God. In one of his prayers, he said: "Lord our Lord, your name is the most wonderful name in all the earth!" (Ps. 8:1 NCV). Other times he just wanted to thank God: "Give thanks to him. . . . For the Lord is always good. He is always loving and kind, and his faithfulness goes on and on" (Ps. 100:4–5 TLB).

This understanding of prayer—simple communication with God—is the common understanding of prayer. Most people think prayer is sending God a fax, leaving Him a message on His voice mail, dialing Him up and telling Him what we want Him to know.

This raises one of the biggest questions that people ask about prayer: Why should I pray when God already *knows* that I'm thankful or that I need help? The answer is that prayer is not simply communication—it is a *relational* event. It's not just the transmission of information—it's a time when you as a child go to your Father in heaven and tell Him about your day. And the Bible clearly teaches that God has chosen to act in response to people's prayers. He has chosen to invest His power and channel His strength in direct relation to people calling out to Him. Beware of the mind-set that says, "Why should I pray? God is going to do what God is going to do," because God says that our prayers matter. Prayer does not *control* God. But He has said that when we pray, we invite His involvement into our lives.

Prayer Is Conversation

Prayer is not simply communication with God; it is a *conversation* with God. Prayer is more than just a monologue; it's a dialogue. We think of prayer as the time when we talk. But what if God has something to say to us? Now I don't mean to suggest that He's going to speak audibly, though He could (and if He did, I'd certainly listen). But God does speak. The way God tends to talk to us is quietly, through our spirits, in a still, small voice. When we pray, we focus our thoughts on God. When we do that, we come in tune with all that He is and all that He might want to say to us. This is the idea behind the words to the song recorded in the Forty-sixth Psalm: "Be quiet and know that I am God" (v. 10 NCV). The phrase "be quiet" means to let go, to cease, to stand still. It speaks of stopping long enough to focus in on God and hear what He might be saying. One writer in the Bible put it this way: "I pray . . . and wait for what he'll say and do" (Ps. 130:6 MSG).

Prayer Is Communion

When I quiet myself and begin to pray—not just talking to God, but trying to reflect silently on God and all that He is and has done, I gain a clarity of thought and an insight into life that comes at no other time and in no other way. Through the dynamic of prayer, we can gain crystal-clear impressions of God's leading, God's wisdom, and God's direction. God wants to engage us, to talk to us, and to make Himself known to us. Prayer opens the door for *communion* with God. Prayer is when we are *with* God, actually in His presence, *experiencing* Him. The Bible says that "the LORD our God comes near when we pray to him" (Deut. 4:7 NCV). And in the Book of James, the Bible says, "Come near to God and he will come near to you" (4:8).

Does entering into God's presence and having communion with Him sound overly mystical to you? It's really not. Many of us have experienced communion with another person; we just didn't think of it that way.

A few years ago, I combined my annual study break with a stint as a visiting professor at the seminary I attended. One night, my oldest daughter and I went for a walk around my old campus. Hand in hand, we strolled around the buildings while I pointed out different places and told her old stories. Then we went into the library where I had spent so many hours. I showed her my former office as a graduate student and a wonderful little reading room where I would go to study. As we entered, we had the room all to ourselves. Closing the door behind us, silence descended. We walked over to a couch and sat down. I put my arm around my daughter's shoulders, but we said nothing. Through the windows, the sun began to set.

56

And for the next fifteen to twenty minutes, we sat in absolute silence, side by side. We were simply *with* each other. We had moved beyond conversation, beyond communication, into communion.

This is something along the lines of what Brother Lawrence, a cook in a seventeenth-century monastery whose devotional writings have influenced many, meant when he wrote that "we should fix ourselves firmly in the presence of God."[4] In fact, Lawrence wrote of reaching the point where he realized that God is intimately present at any given moment. "If I were a preacher," he wrote, "I should preach nothing else but the practice of the presence of God."[5]

How to Pray

So how do you actually do this? During Jesus' teaching ministry, He outlined how to pray. And what He taught was intriguing, because He didn't say anything about a particular place we had to go to pray. He didn't say anything about a specific day or time. He didn't say anything about how you should dress. He didn't say anything about whether you should stand or sit, kneel or lie down. He never mentioned whether you should close your eyes, talk in your head, or speak out loud. So what did He say? Take a look:

This, then, is how you should pray:
"Our Father in heaven:
May your holy name be honored;
may your Kingdom come;
may your will be done on earth as it is in heaven.
Give us today the food we need.

Forgive us the wrongs we have done,
        as we forgive the wrongs that others have done to us.
Do not bring us to hard testing,
        but keep us safe from the Evil One." (Matt. 6:9–13 TEV)

That model prayer is often called "the Lord's Prayer." Jesus never meant it to be a formula or something we repeat word for word like a magical spell. He meant it as a guideline. In essence, He was saying, "Pray like this" or "Pray along these lines." And praying like that involves seven very specific dynamics.

Intimacy

First, Jesus taught that when we talk to God in prayer, we should be intimate. Jesus started His example on how to pray by saying, "Our Father" (v. 9 TEV). That may not seem particularly important, but the word He used for "Father" was the Aramaic word *Abba,* an affectionate term used between small children and their fathers. The best English translation is the word *Daddy.*

Now that's intimate!

I am a father. I know how I feel for my four children. As I once read in a Tony Campolo joke, I couldn't imagine one of them coming to me, standing at attention, saluting me, and saying, "Oh glorious potentate, founder of this family, the one who doth clothe me, feed me, and provide me with every good and perfect gift, might I crawleth on thy lap in order to snuggle?"[6] When I come home, it's a mass attack, with screams of "Daddy's home!" And when it comes time to get in my lap, my children's words are simply, "Daddy, hold me." I wouldn't want it any other way. Neither would God.

Expectancy

Second, Jesus lets us know that when we pray, we should be expectant. When we call out to God, it's not just "Our Father," but "Our Father *in heaven*." God is in heaven—and He is all-powerful, all-knowing, and ever-present. So when we pray, we should pray with a sense of expectancy, knowing that the God to whom we pray is the God who can *act*.

Some people struggle with expecting God to act. A man was walking along a narrow path, not paying much attention to where he was going. Suddenly he slipped over the edge of a cliff. As he fell, he grabbed a branch growing from the side of a cliff. Realizing that he couldn't hang on for long, he called for help: "Is anybody up there?"

Suddenly a voice came down to him. "Yes, I'm here."

The man said, "Who are you?"

The voice said, "I am the Lord."

So the man said, "Lord, help me!"

The Lord said, "Do you trust Me?"

The man said, "Yes! Yes! I trust You completely, Lord!"

Then the Lord said, "Good. Let go of the branch."

The man said, "What?"

The Lord answered, "I said, 'Let go of the branch.'"

After a long pause, the man said, "Is anybody else up there?"

On the other hand, some people have *no* problem with expecting God to act. I once read of a woman who always wanted to get married and have kids but went through her twenties single. She didn't get married until she was thirty-one. She said, "I didn't worry about getting married; I just left my future to God's will. But every night I hung a pair of men's pants on the bed and knelt down and prayed:

> Father in heaven, hear my prayer
> and grant it if You can.
> I've hung a pair of trousers here;
> please fill them with a man!"

Now God may not fill the pants by your bed, but He *can* intervene and make a difference in your life. A lot of us have incredible burdens and problems that are overwhelming to us, but we don't ask God for help. It's as if somewhere deep inside we don't believe God has the power to do anything about it. But Jesus wants us to pray in a way that believes God can do anything, because He *can*—and He's just waiting for us to recognize His power and ask for His help. When we invest our energies into something, that's all it is—our energies. But when we pray, we invite God's activity, God's power, and God's energies.

Reverence

The third lesson we learn from Jesus is that when we pray, we should be reverent. This is the idea behind praying, "May your holy name be honored" (v. 9 TEV). The name of God represents God Himself. We should pray in such a way that God is honored, lifted up, and respected. So while our prayers should be intimate and expectant, they should never be cavalier. We should be honest, but never trite; natural, but never careless, casual, or nonchalant. Jesus wants us to remember that God is God and to interact with Him accordingly—not in fear, but in reverence and in honor.

Submission

Fourth, when we talk to God, we should be submitted to Him. Jesus said to pray with an attitude that says, "May your Kingdom come; may your will be done on earth as it is in heaven" (v. 10 TEV).

Jesus is teaching us to pray in a way that is searching out what God wants and what God cares about. The goal is to find out what God is doing and then to join Him, bringing our lives into alignment with His will. And that's an important lesson on how to pray, because I know my tendency is to try to get God to do what I want or to bless what I've already made up my mind to do!

I once heard about a man who was on a diet. He decided to take a different way to work in the morning, because on his old route he would drive right by a bakery, and it had become his habit to stop and eat when he knew he shouldn't. One day he went into work with a huge coffeecake, and his coworkers asked him if he had stopped trying to lose weight.

He said, "No, I'm just following the will of God!"

They exclaimed, "What do you mean you're following the will of God!"

He said, "Well, you see, I *accidentally* drove by the bakery this morning on the way to work, and this coffeecake was in the window.

I couldn't believe that it was by chance, so I prayed: 'Lord, if you want me to have that coffeecake, let me have a parking space directly in front of the bakery.' And sure enough, the eighth time around the block, there it was!" Praying for the will of God means just that—God's will, not ours.

Think of it like a sailboat. The first time my wife and I traveled to New Zealand, we spent a weekend with a couple who owned a sailboat (which isn't surprising, since there are more sailboats per capita in New Zealand than anywhere else in the world). I had never really sailed before, so our friends took me out and gave me my first real lesson. I learned about the different sails, how to tack, and, most importantly, when to duck. But the heart of sailing soon became clear: You have to find the wind. Only when you find the wind can you fill your sails and make your way. That's how we should pray—searching for what God is doing and wanting, so that we can align ourselves with Him. This means when we pray, we should be open about asking for His guidance and direction—not in a way that is just a smoke screen for getting the coffeecake out of the window, but in order to find the wind to fill our sails.

Dependency

This leads us to the fifth thing that Jesus taught us about prayer—that when we pray, we should be dependent upon God, feeling the freedom to come to God and ask Him to supply our daily needs. Look at how simple and blunt the language Jesus suggests is: "[God,] give us today the food we need" (v. 11 TEV).

But we shouldn't only come to God for food; we should depend upon Him for every area of our lives. We should also say, "Give me today the insight and patience I need to raise my children. Give me today the sensitivity and commitment I need for my marriage. Give me today the money I need, the job that I need, the knowledge I need, the strength that I need." This prayer is not in a spirit that demands, but a spirit that depends.

Honesty

The next lesson Jesus gives is that when we talk to God, we should be honest. Jesus says we should pray that God would "forgive us the wrongs we have done, as we forgive the wrongs that others have done to us" (v. 12 TEV).

Being honest when we talk to God means that we don't try to play games with who we are or what we've done. God knows the junk in our lives—He just wants to see if we'll be authentic enough to *own* it. If we will be honest enough to say, "God, there are some ways that I have really screwed up. I've done some things, said some things, thought some things, and felt some things that I know did not please You. And I need to come clean with You about them. I want to own them and confess each of them to You—without games, excuses, or rationalizations. I am very sorry, and I ask for Your forgiveness." When you do that, you're praying the way Jesus said you should.

Spiritual Realism

The final lesson Jesus gives through His model prayer is that when we pray, we should be spiritual realists. Notice how His model prayer ends: "Do not bring us to hard testing, but keep us safe from the Evil One" (v. 13 TEV).

When we pray, we should be under no illusions about the nature of what we're up against. Every day we will be tempted to do things that will embarrass God: thoughts and actions that will move us away from Him rather than closer to Him. As a result, we are in desperate need of God's help to live the way we're supposed to live. And then there is the reality of the evil one. Jesus said if we are going to pray in a way that is spiritually realistic, we will pray that we will be kept safe from the evil one, who clocks in every morning with one and only one agenda—our failure.

In the Book of Ephesians, the Bible discusses this in very frank language:

> Be strong in the Lord and in his mighty power. Put on the full armor of God so that you can take your stand against the devil's schemes. For our struggle is not against flesh and blood, but against the rulers, against the authorities, against the powers of this dark world and against the spiritual forces of evil in the heavenly realms. Therefore put on the full armor of God, so that when the day of evil comes, you may be able to stand your ground. (6:10–13)

Do you believe in Satan? Many of you may not. Jesus did. He didn't think the devil was a myth. Jesus didn't think Satan was a figment of someone's imagination or a cartoon character. He didn't think the evil one was a mere projection of our minds in order to explain away the mysteries of evil. Jesus believed him to be a real, live spiritual being. He took Satan very, very seriously, and He wanted His followers to take him seriously as well. But that's not what Satan wants. He is very content to have the modern world write him off as a fairy tale. As C. S. Lewis once reminded his readers, there are two equal and opposite errors into which the human race can fall about demons: "One is to disbelieve in their existence. The other is to believe, and to feel an excessive and unhealthy interest in them. They themselves are equally pleased by both errors."[8] Your prayers should be spiritually realistic. This means that when you pray, you will ask God to help you resist the temptations that will come your way to keep you from living the life He's called you to pursue. And not only that, but pray that you will be protected from the schemes of the evil one, whose one and only agenda is to get you off track in your relationship with God.

What Happens When We Pray?

We have been taught that there is a direct relationship between input and output. If we work a certain number of hours, we expect to reach a certain level of success. If we put our kids in the right schools, enroll them in the right programs, and do the right things as parents, we expect them to *turn out* right. If we invest our money strategically and wisely, we expect a fair return on our investment. Input and output. Cause and effect. The relationship between what I do and what actually takes place.

Is this what happens when we pray? Some people do not appear to think so. Author Anne Lamott writes of a friend who says for her morning prayer, "Whatever," and then for the evening, "Oh, well."[9] The Bible encourages a slightly different attitude.

God Hears

First, when you talk to God, He hears you. He listens to you. When you dial, He always picks up.

Bill Gates is one of the richest and most well-known men in the world. And, as you would expect from the founder of the computer giant Microsoft, Gates is on the Internet. But one time *The New Yorker* published his e-mail address. Before he even knew what had happened, Gates began receiving thousands and thousands of messages. So he had to arm his computer with software that now filters through his e-mail, allowing important messages to get through and sending others into electronic oblivion. People wanted to get through to Gates, but he didn't want them to get through to him.[10] Not so with God—He doesn't filter anyone out. The Bible says, "This is the confidence we have in approaching God . . . he hears us" (1 John 5:14).

God Cares

The second thing that happens when you pray is that God cares. You matter to Him. Your problems, your concerns, your worries, and your fears are important to Him. Look at this promise from the Bible: "Let [God] have all your worries and cares, for he is always thinking about you and watching everything that concerns you" (1 Pet. 5:7 TLB). So when you pray, God hears, and God cares.

God Answers

The third thing the Bible says happens when you pray is that God answers every one of your prayers. There is no such thing as unanswered prayer.

Now some of you reading this are thinking, *Okay, now I've got you. I know that isn't true. I specifically prayed for a Maserati sports car, and it's not sitting in my driveway, so I know God doesn't answer every prayer. Once I prayed that I could get to work on time, and I got a flat tire. I pray over the magazine sweepstakes—annually!—and nobody has rung my doorbell with a check. So don't tell me God answers every prayer. He doesn't—and I've got the list to prove it.*

The problem with that line of thinking is that it is based on the idea that prayer is only answered when it is answered the way we *want* it answered. It's as if we say, "God, here is my shopping list, and if You don't come back with everything on it, then You obviously didn't choose to respond." The truth is that God does respond to every prayer. *How* He chooses to respond is another matter. Essentially, there are four ways God might choose to answer your prayers.[11]

When God Says, "No"

First, if the *request* is wrong, God says no. In other words, some prayer requests—no matter how well-intentioned—are inappropriate. Let's look at an example: "The mother of the Zebedee brothers [James and John] came with her two sons and knelt before Jesus with a request. 'What do you want?' Jesus asked. She said, 'Give your word that these two sons of mine will be awarded the highest places of honor in your kingdom, one at your right hand, one at your left hand.' Jesus responded, 'You have no idea what you're asking'" (Matt. 20:20–22 MSG).

The request was heard. Jesus obviously cared for her sons—they were two of His disciples! But the answer was no.

James and John seemed to have a knack for wrong requests. Jesus and His followers were traveling to Jerusalem. One of the cities they had to go through was Samaria. Look at what happened: They "went into a Samaritan village to get things ready for him; but the people there did not welcome him. . . . When the disciples James and John saw this, they asked, 'Lord, do you want us to call fire down from heaven to destroy them?'" (Luke 9:52–54).

James and John were very sincere. They felt the request made sense in terms of what had happened. But notice how Jesus answered: "Jesus turned on them: 'Of course not!'" (v. 55 MSG).

Just because God hears every request and cares deeply about us does not mean His answer can't be no. I know this is true when it comes to my role as a father with my kids. Nobody loves them more than I do. Nobody *cares* about them more than I do. But sometimes when they ask for something, the answer is no. And they don't have a clue why! It makes perfect sense to their minds to stay up all night, to eat ice cream for every meal, to invest significant amounts of our financial resources into the profit margin of Toys "R" Us, and to establish residence at Chuck E. Cheese's pizza—preferably the Orlando location. Could it be that we are to God like our kids are to us? Is it possible that we could make requests that make perfect sense to us but in reality are shortsighted, immature, and self-serving?

Things that are just not *best* for us? If so, then God might just love us too much to give us what we want.

You might be thinking, *I'm with you on how God could say no to some things, but how could it be best that somebody suffer or even die? All I prayed for was that they would get well! How can that be a bad request?* I think that's a legitimate question. Sometimes there is nothing less than a mystery surrounding God's answers to our prayers. I've had times in my life when no matter how I look at the request, there doesn't seem to be anything wrong with it. But God's answer is still no. But I do know that God knows more than I do, and ultimately, I have to settle it within myself as a matter of trust. It all comes down to how you view the character of God. Either He's a good God, or He's not. Either He can be trusted, or He can't. When God seems to say no, you either believe He knows best, or you believe He doesn't. I've often shared with people a simple truth that I believe with all my heart: Nothing happens to you as a Christian that does not first pass through the hands of a God wildly in love with you who will bring all things in line with His purposes. So while we may not understand it or know the reasons for how God responds, we can trust Him, because He loves us more than we can possibly imagine.[12]

When God Says, "Slow"

A second way God can respond to your prayers is this: If the *timing* is wrong, God can say, "Slow." We may think we know the best time for something to happen, but only God knows the *perfect* timing for our lives. And sometimes when we make a request, God says, "Not now."

Now that's tough, because we've gotten used to immediate responses. Companies live and die on how fast they can serve our needs. We can't imagine a life without supermarket express lanes, ATM machines, faxes, cellular phones, and pictures developed in less than an hour. I've heard people reflect on how the words *later* or *not yet* are even worse to hear than *no.*

When God seems to move a bit slow for us, we say, "You don't understand the nature of this situation. I've got this deadline, this reality, these circumstances, so I need to hear from You *today!* Not a year from now, a month from now, or a week from now—but NOW!" And if God doesn't respond immediately, we think He hasn't responded at all. It doesn't enter our thinking that God's timetable is better than ours or that He has information about the situation we don't have. As God said through the prophet Isaiah: "My thoughts are not your thoughts, neither are your ways my ways. . . . As the heavens are higher than the earth, so are my ways higher than your ways and my thoughts than your thoughts" (Isa. 55:8–9). And God's delays are not necessarily God's denials. He has reasons for His "Not yets."[13] God says, "Trust Me. I know what I'm doing."

When God Says, "Grow"

But there's a third way God can answer our prayers. If *you* are wrong, God might say, "Grow." It is possible that something is wrong in our lives, that choices we've made, attitudes we have, and lifestyles we've embraced have set up a barrier between us and God. This is hard to think about, because when it appears God isn't answering our prayers, or answering them the way we want Him to, we automatically think that the problem lies with God. But what if the problem is with us?

Let me offer a few examples of "prayer busters"—actions and attitudes that can interfere with the role of prayer in your spiritual life.[14] The first and most obvious prayer buster is *prayerlessness.* The Bible says, "You do not have, because you do not ask God" (James 4:2). I know that there are a lot of times I have something in my life that I need to be praying about or a need that requires God's supernatural assistance, but I really don't pray about it very much. Or I have a problem and I spend enormous amounts of energy reading self-help books, going to seminars, listening to tapes, and talking to people about it, but I don't invest much energy in actually praying about it.

A second prayer buster is *unconfessed sin.* Look at what the Bible has to say about this: "Your iniquities have separated you from your God; your sins have hidden his face from you, so that he will not hear" (Isa. 59:2). Unconfessed, unconfronted, and unrepentant sin disrupts our intimacy with God and, as a result, interrupts our communication with God.

The sport of NASCAR racing is growing in popularity, and some of the NASCAR drivers, along with many others associated with the sport, attend the church I pastor. But I have a secret confession to make. If you can't dribble it or kick it, I don't get it. But I do know this from my racing friends: Cars need pure fuel. Any contaminant in the fuel will keep the engine from operating at its fullest potential. A speck of dirt could cause a loss of power. It's no different with sin in your life. Your Christian life will not reach its potential if you tolerate sin. It will contaminate your prayers, and the power of your prayer will be diminished.

A third barrier for prayer is *unresolved relational conflict.* Jesus said: "If you are offering your gift at the altar and there remember that your brother has something against you, leave your gift there in front of the altar. First go and be reconciled to your brother; then come and offer your gift" (Matt. 5:23–24).

I think a lot of us grossly underestimate how important community is to God. He wants us to be in healthy relationships. There will be disagreements and conflicts we have to work through, but we are to do it in the context of love. We are to work through disagreements and personality conflicts without attacking the other person or creating division. Now I realize that restoring the relationship isn't always possible. Some people refuse to reconcile with you. But you must do everything you can to resolve the conflict. As the apostle Paul wrote, "If it is possible, as far as it depends on you, live at peace with everyone" (Rom. 12:18). If you refuse to reconcile, then that strained or broken relationship can stand between you and God.

A fourth prayer buster is *selfishness.* The Bible says, "When you ask, you do not receive, because you ask with wrong motives, that you may spend what you get on your pleasures" (James 4:3). If your prayers are along the lines of "Make me famous, make me rich, make all my dreams come true, and always give me the best parking spaces," you probably aren't connecting very well with the Spirit of God. Our tendency is to pray for a trouble-free life, instead of praying that God would mold us into the man or woman He wants us to be.

It's not that God doesn't want us to have a pleasant life, just that pleasantness should not be our main agenda. I once heard of an old legend from a small town in Germany that experienced very poor harvests for a number of years. Finally those townspeople went to God at the beginning of the year and said, "God, our harvests have been so poor and so scarce. For one year will You let us plan everything?"

God said, "All right, for one year."

And so whenever they asked for rain, God sent rain. Whenever they asked for sun, God sent sun. The corn never grew higher, and the wheat never grew thicker. When harvest came, they discovered that the tall corn had no ear, and the thick wheat had no head of grain.

They cried out, "God, You have failed us. We asked for sun, and You sent sun. We asked for rain, and You sent rain. But there is no crop."

God said, "No. You never asked for the harsh north winds. Without the harsh north winds, there is no pollination, and with no pollination, there is no crop."

In contrast, note the spirit of this prayer, written by a Confederate soldier during the Civil War:

> *I asked God for strength, that I might achieve,*
> *I was made weak, that I might learn humbly to obey.*
> *I asked for health, that I might do great things,*
> *I was given infirmity, that I might do better things.*

I asked for riches, that I might be happy,

I was given poverty, that I might be wise.

I asked for power, that I might have the praise of men,

I was given weakness, that I might feel the need of God.

I asked for all things, that I might enjoy life,

I was given life, that I might enjoy all things.

I got nothing that I asked for, but everything that I had
hoped for.

Almost despite myself, my unspoken prayers were answered.

I am, among all men, most richly blessed.[15]

The last prayer buster I'll mention is *inadequate faith.* The Bible says: "If any of you lacks wisdom, he should ask God, who gives generously to all without finding fault, and it will be given to him. But when he asks, he must believe and not doubt, because he who doubts is like a wave of the sea, blown and tossed by the wind. That man should not think he will receive anything from the Lord" (James 1:5–7).

If your heart is filled with doubt, then your prayers will be powerless. The more you are *convinced* of God's ability, the more He will *demonstrate* His ability to you.[16]

When God Says, "Go"

So when God replies to our prayers, if the request is wrong, the answer can be "No." If the timing is wrong, the answer will be "Slow." If we are wrong, the answer will probably be "Grow." But if the request is right, the timing is right, and you are right, God says, "Go!" That is the fourth way God might reply, and nothing pleases God more than to give you the desires of your heart. God hears. God cares. *And God answers.* When our request honors Him, the timing is right, and we are living right, God can and will meet our needs and grant our requests. Skeptics might argue that such events are only coincidences, but as an English archbishop once observed, "It's amazing how many coincidences occur when one begins to pray."[17]

1. Believers have the amazing privilege of talking directly to God in prayer. How does that make you feel?

2. How would you answer someone who asked you, "Why should I pray?"

3. Prayer can include asking God for forgiveness, thanking God, and asking God for help with problems in life. Which of these three aspects of prayer is most meaningful to you and why?

4. What about God makes you want to praise Him?

Chapter Five

Spending Time with God

It's no secret that when it comes to relationships, there is a direct link between time and intimacy. Your closeness to someone is tied to how much time you spend with him or her. If you spend five minutes a month with someone, then you're five-minutes-a-month close. If you spend five minutes a day with someone, then you're five-minutes-a-day close. I'm much more intimate with someone whom I see every day than with someone I see once or twice a year. It's no different with God. If you want to develop your relationship with Him, you have to spend time with Him. And the more time you spend with Him, the closer you'll be to Him and the more your relationship will be developed.

What Jesus Did

Let's start to explore this subject by taking a look at a scene from the life of Jesus that gives us an inside glimpse into what He did to spend time with the Father: "Very early in the morning, while it was still dark, Jesus got up, left the house and went off to a solitary place, where he prayed. Simon and his companions went to look for him, and when they found him, they exclaimed: 'Everyone is looking for you!'" (Mark 1:35–37).

The first thing we notice about Jesus is that He began the day with God. His life was marked by rising early enough to start His day oriented toward God. The second thing we notice is that His time with the Father was *quality* time, involving silence and solitude. This practice seemed to mark the life of Jesus, for in another section of the Bible, we read that "Jesus often slipped away to be alone so he could pray" (Luke 5:16 NCV).

And once alone, surrounded by quiet, Jesus prayed, and evidently would study and reflect upon the Scriptures. This last component is something of an inference from His life, but it is a very compelling one. When Jesus was tempted by Satan, His response was always the same: "It is written. . . . It is written. . . . It is written" (Matt. 4:4, 7, 10). When He talked with people, one of His most frequent questions was: "Haven't you read this scripture?" (Mark 12:10). When asked a question, He would often deal with it in the way described in Luke's Gospel: "Then Jesus quoted them passage after passage from the writings of the prophets, beginning with the book of Genesis and going right on through the Scriptures, explaining what the passages meant" (24:27 TLB).

And the impact of Jesus' time with the Father was profound. Take another look at our glimpse into His life, coupled with His response: "Very early in the morning, while it was still dark, Jesus

78

got up, left the house and went off to a solitary place, where he prayed. Simon and his companions went to look for him, and when they found him, they exclaimed: 'Everyone is looking for you!' Jesus replied, 'Let us go somewhere else—to the nearby villages—so I can preach there also. That is why I have come.' So he traveled throughout Galilee, preaching in their synagogues and driving out demons" (Mark 1:35–39).

Jesus was impacted in three distinct ways as a result of His time with the Father. First, Jesus became *redirected.* He said, "Let us go somewhere else." He gained a clear, fresh understanding of the Father's will for His life. It became clear what He was to do and where He was to go. Second, Jesus became *refueled.* He was eager to travel to the nearby villages "so I can preach there also." He was ready for new tasks, new challenges. Before, His spiritual tanks were running low; after His time with God the Father, He was refueled and ready to continue on with His mission. Third, Jesus became *resolved,* committed to the big picture of His priorities and life purpose. With new clarity, He could say, "This is why I have come."[1]

QUIET TIMES

Following the model of Jesus, countless numbers of Christians desiring to develop their spiritual lives have invested in regular, often daily "quiet times" with God. They've set aside quality time to invest in their relationships with God through prayer and reflection on the Scriptures. They join with the psalmist, who wrote, "Every morning I lay out the pieces of my life on your altar"

(Ps. 5:3 MSG). So let's examine what this would involve. If you were to take time to be with God, what would you actually *do?* You would begin with solitude and silence.

Solitude and Silence

In the movie *Nell,* Jodie Foster plays a young girl whose mother dies. After her mother's death, Nell grows up alone in a forest, divorced from the world and its influences. She is discovered and taken out of the forest by well-meaning people who believe it is best for her to be transitioned back into the world from which she has been isolated.

As the movie develops, Nell's fate is placed into the hands of twelve jurors. After lawyers from both sides finish their closing arguments, Nell herself addresses the jury in the primitive speech she learned as a young child.

"Yo' ha' erna lay," she begins.

"You have big things," another woman translates.

"Yo known'n erna lay."

"You know big things."

Then, leaning toward the jury, gripping the rail that separates them, she says, *"Ma' you'nay seen inna alo'sees."*

"But you don't look into each other's eyes."

Then the intensity of her voice rises. *"An yo'aken of a lilta-lilt."*

"And you're hungry for quietness."

Then, taking a breath as she seemingly searches for the right words, Nell continues, saying through the translator, "I've lived a small life. And I know small things. But the quiet forest is full of angels. In the daytime, there comes beauty. In the nighttime, there comes happiness. Don't be afraid for Nell. Don't weep for Nell."

As Ken Gire has observed, Nell is right. We shouldn't weep for her. We should weep for ourselves. We have big things, we know big things, but we don't look into each other's eyes. And we're hungry for quietness.[2] Thomas Kelly writes of the need to go into "recreating silences."[3] This is what we should allow our quiet times to afford us—*quiet*. We need it.

I played basketball all through junior high and high school, and even some into college, hoping to be a walk-on at my university. And then I worked my way through the first part of my graduate school years by coaching basketball. Having been coached for many years and then serving as a coach, I have come to the conclusion that one of the most significant, powerful, important skills that a coach can possess is knowing when to call a time-out. There is no doubt in my mind that this ability can determine whether the game is won or lost. When you are out on the court as a player, the action is fast and furious. There isn't a lot of time to think or reflect. You just start reacting. And if things start to go poorly, if the shots don't fall or the other team starts to gain the advantage, there's not a lot you can do to change things out on the court except to try to run and jump and play *harder*.

And that takes energy—a lot of energy. Pretty soon, your legs feel like they're made out of lead. And then you get sloppy and start making all kinds of mistakes. It's at that point that a good coach will call a time-out. He'll stop the game, and everybody will get a chance to rest, reflect, and regroup. And then, after the time-out, you're able to go back onto the court and pick up the game where you left off. Only now, you're able to play a little better, a little smarter, and a little sharper. It's become a different game.

In many ways, this is not only the idea behind a quiet time, but it's also the idea behind the Sabbath rest. The Sabbath was about calling for time-out in your life. In the fourth of the famed Ten Commandments, God says, "Remember the Sabbath day by keeping it holy. Six days you shall labor and do all your work, but the seventh day is a Sabbath to the LORD your God. On it you shall not do any work" (Exod. 20:8–10). The Word *Sabbath* doesn't mean Sunday or Saturday. It literally means to cease—to stop, to quit, to rest. And the word *holy* means to be something different, set apart, unique, unlike anything else. So the Fourth Commandment is clear: Every seven days, call a time-out. Stop the game. And then use that time for a real Sabbath, a rest that will serve both you and your relationship with God.

And this rest is important. Work and busyness and fast-paced schedules are at war against the deep issues of your life. As I mentioned earlier, I've always been intrigued by what God says in the Forty-sixth Psalm: "Be still, and know that I am God" (v. 10). How do you know God? You have to be still. Life is meant to be lived on two levels—the level of outward activities and the level of the interior life.[4] The temptation is to live on one level alone. This is why you have to stop long enough to let God speak to you, reveal Himself to you, and engage you. This is also why coupling silence with solitude is so powerful. As Samuel Chadwick once observed,

"It would revolutionize the lives of most [people] if they were shut in with God in some secret place for half an hour a day."[5]

There's a fascinating story from the pages of African colonial history. As told by Lettie Cowman, a traveler was taking a long journey and had enlisted some of the local tribesmen to assist him in carrying his loads. The first day, they moved fast and went far. But on the second day, the jungle tribesmen refused to move. They just sat and rested. The traveler, who wanted to get on with his journey, asked them why they wouldn't keep going. They told him that they had gone too fast on the first day and that they were now *waiting for their souls to catch up with their bodies.*[6] Mrs. Cowman makes the following conclusion: "The whirling, rushing life which so many of us live does for us what that first march did for those poor jungle tribesmen. The difference: *They knew* what they needed to restore life's balance; too often *we do not.*"[7]

Reflection and Meditation

But silence and solitude—for their own sake—will not nourish your soul nor enliven your intimacy with God. Your time with God must have content, purpose, and direction. This is the difference between Christian meditation and many forms of Eastern meditation. For the Buddhist, the goal is to empty the soul. For the Christian, the goal is to *fill* it. We must go from *detachment* to *attachment.*[8] As Dietrich Bonhoeffer once wrote, silence is "nothing else but waiting for God's Word and coming from God's Word with a blessing."[9]

This involves three primary activities: reading the Word of God, reflecting on the Word of God, and then responding to the Word of God. *Reading* simply involves using your eyes to take in what is on the surface.[10] *Reflecting* on the Word of God engages your mind to see what is beneath the surface. *Responding* to the Word of God is giving what we have seen a place to live within our hearts.[11] As Ken Gire has noted, reading the Word without taking time to reflect on it would be like sitting at a table where a sumptuous meal has been prepared and eyeing all the food but never eating. And reflecting upon the Word without prayerfully responding to it would be like chewing the food but never swallowing.[12] The Word of God comes in the "recreating silences," but we must determine whether we will let it "re-create" us.

But if we will read the Bible, the impact on our lives should not be underestimated. The First Psalm notes that the person who leads a blessed life not only delights in the law of the Lord but meditates on it day and night in order that it might guide his steps and serve as his counsel. Result? "He is like a tree planted by streams of water, which yields its fruit in season and whose leaf does not wither. Whatever he does prospers" (v. 3).

But mere silence and solitude, reflection and meditation, is not all. Our time with God must be coupled with active and intent *listening*. As we quiet ourselves and reflect on God's word to us through the Scriptures, we will experience God speaking to our lives. This is more than responding to the Word in terms of obedience. The quieting of your life and heart, coupled with reflection and meditation on the Word of God, will result in God *impressing*

Himself upon you, giving you guidance, direction, prompting, and insight. As the Bible reminds us, "Our God comes and will not be silent" (Ps. 50:3). Few verses are as poignant as those in the first chapter of Proverbs, where God says, "If only you had listened . . . I would have told you what's in my heart; I would have told you what I am thinking. I called, but you refused to listen" (vv. 23–24 NCV).

A way of capturing this "listening" often involves journaling, keeping a written record of thoughts and prayers to God that flow from our quiet times. I confess that I have had a difficult relationship with journaling over the years, feeling almost repulsed by its recorded, almost public nature. I considered myself far too self-conscious to pour out my secret thoughts and feelings on paper, for fear that it would be found and read. I also felt that if I journaled, I would be tempted to write as if one day the journals would be found, perhaps even published posthumously, thereby adopting a false and unrealistic tone to ensure my place in spiritual folklore. Yet I never could quite get away from the *idea* of journaling, however much I may have chafed at the thought of the practice of the discipline. Many Christians have found journaling to be a valuable practice, and many men and women I respect recommend it.

So I began keeping a journal, but on my own terms. For many Christians, journaling is the pouring out of every thought and every prayer, creating a running spiritual diary. For me, it is simply a place to capture what God seems to be trying to tell me, to do with me, and to reveal to me about myself and Himself. When such spiritual insights come, they are precious. In the past, I had scribbled them down on notes, kept them tucked away in a file, on my desk, or in a drawer, but they were soon lost or forgotten. I have come to realize that I simply cannot afford this. I need these insights grouped together, available for review, reflection, remembrance, and, most importantly, continued application.

Prayer

The final component to time with God is prayer. Time with God will always involve communication, conversation, and communion, as discussed in the previous chapter on prayer.[13] This time of prayer can be guided by many things, not the least of which is your response to the Word of God received through your time with the Word, resulting in praise, confession, gratitude, or request. Yet prayer must not simply be responsive—it must also be intentional and proactive. Consider the following four movements.[14]

Praise

You can give God praise for being faithful, just, merciful, gracious, forgiving, generous, tender, loving . . . the list cannot be exhausted. The key is to praise God, not simply to thank Him. There is a difference. Thanking God is expressing gratitude for what God has *done*. Praise is honoring God for who He *is*. Praise is starting off with a heart that says, "I'm praying to an incredible God."

Confession

A second movement involves confession and repentance. This is a time when you walk through your actions, words, thoughts, and deeds and evaluate them in light of God's truth and the presence of the Holy Spirit, letting that evaluation lead you to a time of con-fession and repentance and then asking for forgiveness. Often our time alone with God, reflecting on His Word, has already opened the eyes of our heart anew to who we really are and how we have been living. Take this time to confess attitudes, actions, thoughts, and deeds that did not honor God or failed to reflect your rela-tionship with Him. This is a very important and very healthy enter-prise. It's the key to a cleansed conscience, the experience of forgiveness, and the removal of guilt, and it serves as the gateway to the freedom to pray for God's power and activity in your life.

Gratitude

A third movement relates to gratitude. Take time to thank God for all that He's done for you. We all know what it feels like when someone thanks us for something. And if you have a child, you know that there's no feeling in the world that compares to your child turning to you and saying, "Thanks for doing that, Dad." Or, "Mom, thanks." It just doesn't get any better. It matters between you and God too. He's our Father, and He is moved by our expres-sions of thanksgiving as His children. So thank Him for answered prayers, for the rewards and benefits that come from your relation-ship with Him, for the friends and family you have in your life, and for the material blessings He's brought your way. Just say thanks.

Request

The final movement relates to asking God for things, coming to Him with our personal issues and concerns. Or as the apostle

Paul put it, "In everything, by prayer and petition, with thanksgiving, present your requests to God" (Phil. 4:6). And when the Bible says "everything," it means everything. Nothing is too big for God to handle, and nothing is too small for Him to care about. So pray for people you know, particularly those who are going through a difficult time or have a great deal of responsibility to carry. Pray for your spouse and your children. Ask for help with decisions about finances, education, and time management. Pray about personal things, such as your character or other private issues you may be struggling with. Ask God for help, guidance, and strength.

By the way, a number of acrostics have been developed to help you remember this kind of content for prayer, such as ACTS, representing adoration, confession, thanksgiving, and supplication (intercession); PETAL, for praise, evaluation, thanksgiving, asking, and listening; and PRAYER, for praise, repentance, asking, yielding, evaluating, and reflecting.

BUILDING A QUIET TIME INTO YOUR LIFE

So how do you build this into your life? Enormous help can be found through a man named Daniel, who led an extraordinary life. During his time, Daniel was one of the top three men in the government of the world's largest empire, personally responsible for forty districts of the kingdom, constituting one-third of the entire land. To put ourselves in his shoes, we would need to be personally responsible for governing all of the states in America east of the Mississippi River. And Daniel was so good at his job, so committed and invested, that the king eventually placed him in charge of the *entire* kingdom. Daniel was a very busy man, and he managed his responsibilities with the highest level of effectiveness. Yet look at this passing observation about his schedule: "Daniel . . . went home and knelt down as usual in his upstairs bedroom, with its windows open toward Jerusalem, and prayed three times a day, just as he always had, giving thanks to his God" (Dan. 6:10 TLB).

Daniel was a man who had built a regular quiet time with God into his life. He found time for it, worked it in, and never let it get sidelined, marginalized, or put on the shelf. So how did he do it? First, it would appear that Daniel included his quiet time in his schedule. It wasn't something he left to chance. He prioritized it and wrote it in his Day-Timer. In fact, the Bible tells us that he had three set times a day for it, with a planned place to go and do it. And the Bible makes one other little observation: Not only did he have a specific time and place for his quiet time, but Daniel made an ongoing investment in this time. Did you notice the language? The Bible says that Daniel "went home and knelt down *as usual . . . just as he always had*" (v. 10 TLB; emphasis added). Spending time with God was a pattern for Daniel's life—not in an uptight, legalistic way, but in a disciplined, committed way.

For a long time, I struggled with doing this in my own life. As a pastor, I often felt that I knew more *about* quiet times than I was actually practicing in my life. It always seemed like I was too busy, too preoccupied. But then I became challenged by a simple idea: If I'm too busy for a quiet time, I'm too busy for God! Too busy for His *power,* His *presence,* His life-changing *impact,* and His *leadership.* Then it just became crystal-clear to me: "I'm not too busy to be with God—I'm too busy *not* to be with God."[15] So I took a long look at the life of Daniel, not to mention Jesus, and began applying their lifestyle choices. I started by looking for a time. And the best time I could think of was at the start of the day. It was the habit of Jesus, it was when I was at *my* best, and it would best serve the course of my day.

Then I needed a place. There were many locations I could go to in my house, except for one little problem—actually, *four* little problems—my children! Once they wake up, there can be no such thing as quality time alone with *anybody* to do *anything.* So that meant that if I was going to use a place in the house in the mornings for my quiet time, I would have to get up *before* my kids. So I did. And that began a pattern that has revolutionized my life. I get up about two hours before anyone else—and during that time I pray, read my Bible, have time for coffee and the newspaper, and then go out for my workout at the gym. It's just a rich time—in fact, I often joke that my day goes downhill from that point on—but those two hours are great! It has meant going to bed a little earlier, but that's been a very small price to pay for something that has brought more to my spiritual life than anyone could possibly imagine.

GETTING STARTED

If you want to develop your relationship with God, you need to have a regular quiet time as part of your life. And the most important thing you can do is to get started. Here's how.

First, set aside a *time*. Put it on your calendar. For me, it's early in the morning. That's not for everybody, I know, but the point is for you to set aside an actual place in time to be with God on a regular basis and then make it a part of your schedule. And since this is time for you and God, think in terms of when you are at your best. I have become convinced that there is something about starting the day with God that serves most people well, but the real principle is to make sure it's a time when you are able to have quality time alone with God.

Second, try to find a specific *place* to go for your quiet time. It may be in your office with the door closed. It may be at the kitchen table or in a rocker on your porch. But find a place where you can be alone and uninterrupted.

Third, have a *plan* for your quiet time. Know what you're going to do. And if you're new to this, let me make a suggestion. Start off with just seven minutes. Five minutes is probably too short, and ten minutes may be too long at first, so begin with seven. All of us should be able to manage seven minutes a day with God.

Here's the plan: Set your time—let's say it's first thing in the morning. Know where you are going to go. Then set the alarm.

When it goes off, get yourself up, make the coffee, grab your Bible, and go to the place you have chosen. Once there, invest the first thirty seconds preparing your heart. Maybe just thank God for a good night's sleep or for a new day to live. In that thirty seconds, you might want to ask Him to open your heart so that you can be responsive to what He might say to you through prayer or what you read. Ask Him to be with you, to meet with you, to speak to you, and to teach you.

Just thirty seconds.

Then take your Bible and read it for two or three minutes. Just read it. I would suggest that you start reading one of the biographies of Jesus, like the Gospel of Mark. Then take a couple of minutes to *reflect* on what you have read, including how you might respond. The next day, pick up where you left off. Don't race through your reading, but don't get bogged down either. Read for the joy of reading, and just let God speak to you.

Four minutes total so far.

Each day, after you've spent four minutes reading and reflecting on the Bible, letting God speak to you, spend two and a half minutes in prayer, talking to God. Tell Him what's on your mind, ask for His forgiveness, thank Him for things He's done, and ask Him for what you need or for the needs of others.

Two and a half minutes.

So take thirty seconds preparing your heart and asking for God's presence and guidance; four minutes reading and reflecting on the Bible, listening to His Word to you; then two and a half minutes talking to Him. Seven minutes a day with God.

After a while, you'll discover that seven minutes quickly become ten, and then fifteen; soon you'll be spending the kind of solid, consistent, rich time with God that transforms your life on the deepest levels and develops the kind of intimacy with God you've always wanted.[16]

CONCLUSION

Spending time with God is crucial to your relationship with God, because most relationships are like riding a bike up a hill. Once you stop pedaling, you don't just stop climbing—you start going back down the hill! Or think of time with God like an anchor to a boat. Without it, you begin to drift, slowly at first, away from where you were. But soon you find yourself very far from where you started—and from where you want to be. Your relationship with God must be attended to, cared for, and nurtured. But time with God is not just something that we need; it's also something God desires.

When she was around five years old, my daughter Rebecca would get up early in the morning. When she did, she would get out of her bed and come into Susan's and my bedroom. Then she'd walk over to my side of the bed, tap me on the shoulder, and whisper, "Come be with me, Daddy; come be with me."

I'd usually be asleep, and the last thing I wanted was to get out of bed. But when I heard that soft little voice and opened my eyes to see that precious little girl in her nightgown, wanting to be with her daddy, I just melted. So I'd get up, and Rebecca and I would be together—just the two of us. How could I say no? How can you turn down someone whom you love and who loves you and just wants to spend time with you? Those were priceless times, and they did so much for our relationship. I can't imagine what my life would be like—much less what my relationship with Rebecca would be like—without them.

I think that, every morning, God comes to the side of your bed and beckons, "Come be with Me." And if you'll say yes, you'll be very, very glad.

1. Why is it important for believers to spend time with God each day?

2. What time of day do you find it easiest to concentrate on God?

3. What places do you find most conducive for spending time with God (e.g., a back porch)?

4. Which books of the Bible have meant the most to you, and which would you like to read next?

5. It seems incredible that God really wants us to tell Him exactly what is weighing on our minds. What does that tell you about God?

CHAPTER SIX

The New Community

The first time I traveled to the famed American port city of Boston, I built time into my schedule to tour its well-known sites. I followed the famous Red Line through the heart of the city's historical district, made my way to the waterfront, walked the naval yard where my father had been stationed during the Korean War, and spent some time at the Commons. But I confess that what I *really* wanted to find was a bar! The Bull and Finch Restaurant and Bar, to be exact. You may know it by another name—Cheers. The Bull and Finch was the inspiration for the hit TV series *Cheers,* which was one of my favorite shows; so while I was in Boston, I wanted to see the real thing. And I did. I went in, ate lunch, and had a great time.

As I was walking out, I began to think about all of the things that made me like that series—the memorable characters, the funny stories, the great one-liners. But it clicked with me that what I liked most was something deeper. In truth, I was drawn to the sense of *community.* At Cheers, everybody seemed to *care* about each other, *support* each other, and *accept* each other's weaknesses. It was the kind of place you'd like to be able to just go to and hang out.

Remember the theme song?

> *Making your way in the world today*
> *takes everything you've got.*
> *Taking a break from all your worries*
> *sure would help a lot.*
> *Wouldn't you like to get away?*
> *Sometimes you want to go*
> *Where everybody knows your name.*
> *And they're always glad you came.*
> *You want to be where you can see,*
> *our troubles are all the same.*
> *You want to be where everybody knows your name.*[1]

There's something about community—the relationships, the sense of belonging, the support and encouragement, the sympathy and understanding—that deepens our lives and anchors our souls. But the community pictured in TV shows like *Cheers* pales in comparison to the truest, best, clearest picture of community that has ever been presented—the *new* community, better known as the church. And no better snapshot can be found than in the second chapter of Acts:

> They devoted themselves to the apostles' teaching and to
> the fellowship, to the breaking of bread and to prayer.

Everyone was filled with awe, and many wonders and miraculous signs were done by the apostles. All the believers were
together and had everything in common. Selling their possessions and goods, they gave to anyone as he had need.
Every day they continued to meet together in the temple
courts. They broke bread in their homes and ate together
with glad and sincere hearts, praising God and enjoying the
favor of all the people. And the Lord added to their number
daily those who were being saved. (vv. 42–47)

In this portrait, we find that the new community that Christ
came to establish is a place where you can love and be loved,
know and be known, serve and be served, and celebrate and be
celebrated.[2] And those are four things that are *indispensable* to a
spiritual life.

To Love and Be Loved

The first mark of the new community is that it is a place where
you can love and be loved. Luke observed, "They devoted themselves
to the . . . fellowship" (Acts 2:42). The word Luke used for *fellowship*
is the Greek word *koinonia,* which has to do with companionship,
sharing, and being connected with another person in intimacy. It is
the expression of enthusiastic love. People were taking the "high
road" with each other, never assuming the worst or giving in to suspicion. True *koinonia* is when people are completely upheld, completely accepted, and completely supported. "To love a person," said
Dostoevsky, "means to see him as God intended him to be."[3]

To Know and Be Known

But not only did Luke say that they were devoted to the fellowship, he also noted that "all the believers were together and had everything in common" (v. 44). They were sharing, talking, revealing—they were not holding anything back. The truth is that we all have weaknesses. A true community allows you to stand up and say, "My name is John, and I'm an alcoholic; my name is Betty, and I have breast cancer; my name is Steve, and my marriage is falling apart; my name is Bill, and I have AIDS; my name is Carol, and I just lost my job; my name is Alice, and I'm lonely." But community is not simply being able to reveal who we are, but for that revelation to be in *safe hands*. Knowledge of one another in the new community is not the basis for wounding, but healing through the giving and receiving of grace, love, and support.

To Serve and Be Served

The third mark of the new community is that it is a place where you can serve and be served. When Luke described the early church, he noted: "Selling their possessions and goods, they gave to anyone as he had need" (v. 45). There was a spirit of giving to each other at their points of need.

A young woman in our church experienced the horror of being diagnosed with breast cancer. After the cancer was discovered, it was considered advanced enough to require a radical mastectomy. She and her husband quickly became surrounded by prayer and support, phone calls, meals, and all the counsel and advice their network of medical friends and family could provide. It would take hours for me to get through to their home because the line was continually busy with calls from concerned friends. As I drove to visit her husband in the waiting room of the hospital during the surgery, I passed by three members of the church in the parking lot on my way in who had stopped by as well. Later, when I spoke to them about their ordeal, her husband simply said, "I cannot imagine going through this without a church family. It would be so lonely."

To Celebrate and Be Celebrated

A final mark of the new community is that it is where you can celebrate and be celebrated. Notice how Luke ended his summary: "They broke bread in their homes and ate together with glad and sincere hearts, praising God and enjoying the favor of all the people. And the Lord added to their number daily those who were being saved" (vv. 46–47). They were being together and having fun. They were in each other's homes, sharing meals, laughing and talking, enjoying life with each other and with God. It was so good that other folks who weren't even Christians wanted to *be* Christians because of the community!

DISAPPOINTMENT WITH THE CHURCH

Sounds good, doesn't it? But many of you are saying, "That's not the church I know about." You're wanting to say, "Spirituality, yes. Church, no." You have some good reasons for feeling that way.

Ken Blanchard is well known for his book *The One-Minute Manager* and the many "one-minute" applications that followed. Blanchard became a Christian late in his life, and, in writing about that decision, he talked candidly about why he didn't pursue Christianity earlier. As a young man, he was involved in a church near Kent State University during the sixties, when there was a great deal of student unrest. In fact, Kent State was the site of one of the worst moments of that period when the National Guard opened up fire and killed four students. The minister of the church Blanchard attended was sympathetic with the students. He joined them during their protests and their marches. That didn't go over very well with some of the more conservative members of the congregation, so they terminated his employment in a very abrupt and unkind way. Blanchard wrote that anger and disillusionment came crashing in on him. He said, "If that's what church is all about, forget it." He and his wife dropped out, and for the next fifteen years, they attended only at Christmas and Easter.[4]

Related to this is the internal discord within churches that many have encountered. I once came across a very disturbing news story on the front page of a newspaper in Louisville, Kentucky. The headline read: "Church Meeting Ends in Fray, Beleaguered Pastor Resigns Amid Turmoil." The article recounted the tale of the St. Paul Missionary Baptist Church. A story that involved years of discord, division, and turmoil finally erupted one Sunday into fistfights between members that took more than a dozen Louisville police officers to end. The reporter had every right to be sarcastic when he wrote that those "who shortly before had been lifting hands in praise of God began raising hands against one another."[5] And because of that, people look at the church and say, "Thanks, but no thanks. I've got enough problems in my life—I don't need to go to church and get more."

While the church can at times be a dysfunctional expression of the community it was intended to be, it continues to have a clear and compelling vision that shapes it toward health and wholeness in a way unlike any other gathering. Jesus came to establish a *new* community of people. He said, "I will build *my* church" (Matt. 16:18; emphasis added). Jesus wanted the church to be full of people who are allowed and encouraged to be *real* with each other, opening themselves up for care and love and support. The new community that Jesus initiated was to be built on healthy, deep, loving relationships that were being forged on the anvil of conflict resolution. The new community that Jesus came to establish was to be marked by a spirit of *acceptance,* one that looks at people, imperfections and all, and receives them for who they are and how God made them. Most people find that when they explore the vision for church that Jesus and the Bible describes, it isn't church *itself* they are turned off to, but the way people have been *doing* church. And while many churches fall short of this vision, countless others are *decisively* marked by the biblical portrait of the church as the new community. When you find a church like that and invest in it, you will discover the community that you long for and desperately need.[6]

The lie is that we can do life on our own. The truth is that we can't. If we don't bond with people, we become emotionally and spiritually dysfunctional. *Seriously* dysfunctional. The results of one study conducted in 1945 are still fascinating. This study looked at infants in institutions. The physical needs of all of the babies were met. They were fed when they were hungry, and their diapers were changed when they were wet. However, because of the shortage of caretakers, only some of the babies were held and talked to. The ones who were *not* held showed drastically higher rates of illness—and even death. In addition, their psychological development was either slowed or stopped. All because of one thing: a lack of emotional, *relational* bonding.[7]

John Stott tells of a Scottish minister who visited a church member who had drifted away from the community of the church. Upon entering the home, the minister sat down with the man in his den before the fireplace. Neither said a word. Finally, the minister leaned forward, picked up the fireplace tongs, and took a burning coal from the fire. He laid the coal off to the side, and, in just a few moments what was once a bright, burning coal turned to cold, gray ash and eventually went out altogether. Then the minister picked it back and put it with the other coals. Within a few seconds, it was on fire again. Then the minister got up and left the man. Neither said a word through the entire visit, but the point was made. The next weekend, the man had returned to his family of faith.[8]

SIGNING ON

So how do you experience the rewards of the new community? By joining one! You cannot develop yourself spiritually to the degree

God intends apart from others, which is why finding a community—and *committing* to it—is one of the most important spiritual steps you can take.

The Bible teaches that "we who are many are one body in Christ, and individually members one of another" (Rom. 12:5 NIV). Even further, the Bible says that, as a Christian, "you are members of God's very own family, . . . and you belong in God's household with every other Christian" (Eph. 2:19 TLB). That last verse holds three key truths: first, that the church is a family; second, that God expects Christians to be members of a church family; and third, that a Christian without a church family is a contradiction! Not only does becoming a member of a local church community express obedience to the Bible, but it moves us into a position of committed participation. It presents an opportunity to "step out of the stands" and publicly assert our commitment to Christ and to a specific local faith community. In this sense, membership can be one of the most significant and defining moments in your spiritual life. Yet while membership in a church brings you into the new community, it is only the *entrance*. The *power* of relational life must still be seized.

THE POWER OF RELATIONSHIPS

Let's take a little quiz. Clear your desks and put away your books. Take out a pencil and a sheet of paper and write down your answer to this question: If two horses can pull nine thousand pounds, how many pounds can four horses pull?

If you wrote down nine thousand pounds, you were wrong. If you wrote *eighteen thousand* pounds, you were wrong. The answer is that while two horses can pull nine thousand pounds, four horses can pull more than *thirty thousand* pounds. Now if that doesn't make sense, it's because you haven't been introduced to the concept of synergy.

Synergy is the energy or force that is generated through the working together of various parts or processes. In his classic economics text, *The Wealth of Nations,* Adam Smith wrote that ten people working individually can produce twenty pins a day, but ten people working *together* can produce *forty-eight thousand* pins a day. Synergy is bigger than just tasks, production, or the weight you can pull. It has to do with every aspect of life. A married couple will tell you of the benefit of a Christian counselor. An athlete will talk about the importance of a trainer or a coach. A businessperson will talk about the power of a team. And this concept is true for your spiritual life as well. When you start developing strategic, spiritual relationships in your life, the impact is phenomenal. The reason begins with the *challenge* these relationships bring to your life.

Challenge

Nothing pushes me, motivates me, or influences me more than being around someone who is operating at a higher level than I am—someone who is stronger than I am, more developed than I am, has accomplished more than I have, or has a depth of character exceeding my own. When I'm around those kinds of people, it makes me want to commit myself more deeply, pay attention to areas I've ignored, and deepen my walk with God. It makes me want to elevate my game to a new level.

I recently had dinner in the home of a friend of mine who challenges me in this way. He's very well known in the Christian community as a leader, speaker, and author. Although I've met many people in that category, few have struck me the way he does. He's simply a serious player for God, a true competitor. He's in the race not just to survive, but to prevail. To win. To make a difference. He's got a "whatever-it-takes" mentality when it comes to his spiritual life and his commitment to the things of God. Every time I'm with him, I walk away more resolved, more committed, and more determined than ever to give my life wholeheartedly to God. This is the idea behind the Bible's admonition: "As iron sharpens iron, so one man sharpens another" (Prov. 27:17). Iron against iron—the clang, the noise, the sparks, and the contact. You can feel the idea of challenge coming through. And that's what keeps us sharp.

Encouragement

A second payoff from relationships has to do with *encouragement*. The Bible says: "Let us consider how we may spur one another on toward love and good deeds. Let us not give up meeting together, as some are in the habit of doing, but let us encourage one another" (Heb. 10:24–25). We all need people who come alongside us and help us to keep going.

Some time ago I was going through a difficult time. I was tired and emotionally depleted. I don't often talk about such things to others—my tendency is to hold it in and just buck up. But one Wednesday night, at our midweek service, I made a slight reference to my emotional state at the beginning of a talk—just something minor, like "Boy, I needed tonight's worship because, like many of you, I've had a long week, and that was just a shot in the arm." The next day, a friend of mine in the church who is enormously busy with her career as a pediatrician came by my office with a large cup that was stuffed with candy and tied up in ribbons, with a card attached to it. And inside that card, she wrote: "Jim: From what you said last night at church, you are having a rough week. Hope this cheers you up. So many people, including myself, would not be walking with Christ if it weren't for you and your dedication to the mission. Thanks for serving the Lord with your gift of leadership."

I needed that. We all do.

Accountability

Another dynamic that relationships bring is *accountability*. Socrates once contended that the unexamined life was not worth living. It could be said that the unexamined *spiritual* life is not *able* to be lived. And when it comes to our spirituality, only so much is able to be self-inspected. Chuck Colson writes of the power that accountable relationships have brought to his life, particularly his regular gathering with a small group of men for the purpose of sharing and dialogue—conversation that includes asking each other the following seven questions:

1. Have you been with a woman anywhere this past week that might be seen as compromising?

2. Have any of your financial dealings lacked integrity?

3. Have you exposed yourself to any sexually explicit material?

4. Have you spent adequate time in Bible study and prayer?

5. Have you given priority time to your family?

6. Have you fulfilled the mandates of your calling?

7. Have you just lied to me?[9]

Accountability should never become a euphemism for control or for a legalistic, oppressive existence that lives in fear and bondage. It is simply living a life that allows others to see inside so that they can bring objective counsel and helpful challenge.

Support

A final contribution that relationships often bring has to do with support. The Bible says: "Two are better than one, because they have a good return for their work: If one falls down, his friend can help him up. But pity the man who falls and has no one to help him up!" (Eccles. 4:9–10). Challenge is needed. Encouragement is needed. But so is *support*, somebody who can provide help. Someone who can put his arm around you and help you make it through those times you cannot stand on your own.

Henry Cloud tells of a friend of his who called him and said, "Can we have lunch on Thursday?" Henry said, "Sure, I'm free. What's up?"

And his friend said, "I've lost everything. Everything. My money manager has embezzled everything I have, and I'm in trouble. So can you just meet me for lunch on Thursday?" What was particularly heartbreaking was that only a few months earlier, this man's wife had left him and had taken their children with her. So now he was stripped of everything—his wife, his children, and his money.

The day for the lunch came, and Henry found out that his friend had invited others as well, assembling a small group of his closest friends. Once gathered around the table, he said, "Guys, I'm busted. It looks like I have lost everything. It is really bleak. But here's what I need from you. If each of you will sign up for a day a week to have lunch with me, if I know that I will see one of you every day, I can make my comeback. If I know that I have your support, then I can do it."

They all answered that he could count on them, and in about eighteen months, he had done it. He was back on his feet financially and spiritually. But it took some people who were willing just to *live* with him—to go through it with him.[10] Such stories are testimony to Dietrich Bonhoeffer's declaration that simply the "physical presence of other Christians is a source of incomparable joy and strength to the believer."[11] Or as Anne Lamott has written, "no matter how bad I am feeling, how lost or lonely or frightened, when I see the faces of the people at my church, and hear their tawny voices, I can always find my way home."[12]

ADDING RELATIONSHIPS TO YOUR LIFE

So how do you develop strategic spiritual relationships within the new community? Well, it's not going to happen hanging out by the doughnuts and coffeepot every weekend. Bill Hybels caricatures what passes for relational life in most churches with the following interaction between two men at church:

"So how's it going at work, Jake?"

"Fine, Phil. Say, you driving a new car?"

"Used. What do you have going on this week?"

"Not much."

"Well, great fellowshipping with you, Jake."

"Same here."[13]

That's not going to add much to your life. So how *do* you develop the kind of relationships that serve your spiritual life? It begins with taking a *relational inventory.*

Take a Relational Inventory

It has been said that what you will be like in five years is based on two things: the books you read and the people you spend time with. It is difficult to underestimate the impact of the people who surround you.

I once heard one of my college professors make a passing reference to a marketing study of teenagers. Apparently several high-school students were asked to give their opinions regarding a particular style of jeans. Overwhelmingly, the students thought that they were the ugliest jeans they had ever seen! The researchers waited a few months and then went back to the same high school. They took key opinion leaders—the captain of the basketball team, the head cheerleader, the first-string quarterback, the homecoming queen, and the student body president— gave each one a pair of the jeans, and asked them to wear them regularly to school for one month without telling anyone why they were choosing to wear the new style. By the end of the month, stores were besieged by students wanting to know where they could find the new fashion.

The influence of others doesn't diminish as we grow older. Baseball fans are familiar with the name of Casey Stengel, former manager of the New York Yankees. When Billy Martin took over as manager, Stengel had some interesting advice for him. He said, "Billy, on any team there will be fifteen guys who will run through a wall for you, five who will hate you, and five who are undecided." Stengel then said, "When you make out your rooming list, always room your losers together. Never room a good guy with a loser. *It won't spread if you keep them isolated.*" [14]

If you are surrounded by spiritually positive and healthy people, you will find your *own* spiritual life and development boosted. The opposite is equally true—there are those who can actually *weaken* you spiritually, lowering your commitment and resolve. This is the importance of maintaining a relational inventory in your life at all times. This is not meant to exclude people who need our influence. As John Maxwell has wisely pointed out, there is a difference between helping those with perpetual attitude problems and enlisting them as our close friends. The closer our relationship, the more influential their attitudes and philosophies become to us.[15]

Consider the life of Jesus. He cared about everyone, but there were certain people whom He was drawn to relationally. For example, Jesus pulled Peter, James, and John off to the side to be with Him at spiritually important times. It was Peter, James, and John whom Jesus wanted with Him at the high points of His ministry, such as the raising of a little girl from the dead, as well as the transfiguration, where Moses and Elijah came and spoke with Jesus. It was also Peter, James, and John whom Jesus called to be with Him at His most difficult times, such as in the Garden of Gethsemane the night before His crucifixion. You could also make a case that Mary, Martha, and Lazarus were important to Jesus in terms of strategic relationships. An interesting statement in the Gospel of John says, "Jesus loved Martha and her sister [Mary] and Lazarus" (11:5). In fact, Jesus seemed to continually orient His travel plans in order to stay at their house. Jesus modeled life as it was meant to be lived, and He understood that some people *feed* you, and some people feed *off* of you. You need a balance of both for spiritual health.

In taking your own relational inventory, begin with the three basic types of people in your life—those who drain you, those who are neutral, and those who put gas in your spiritual tanks. Gordon MacDonald talks about these categories in terms of

VRPs, "very resourceful people" who serve as mentors and ignite our spiritual passion; VIPs, "very important people" who share our spiritual passion and stand by our side; VNPs, "very nice people" who don't take anything away, but they don't put anything in either; and the VDPs, "very draining people" who impact us adversely.[16] Now one person's VDP may be somebody else's VIP. In the Bible we find that the apostle Paul (at least initially) had a hard time with Mark, while Barnabas gladly invested time and energy into Mark's life. The point is to take an inventory of who these people are for *you*.

Intentionally Find and Develop Mentors

The second step is to use this inventory to intentionally find and develop your relationship with those people who positively impact your spiritual life. Spend time with them. Knit your hearts and lives together. Let them challenge, encourage, and support you, as you do the same for them. And then, look for those that can become even more strategic—those who might be able to become something of a mentor.

Mentoring is how most people used to be trained and developed for life. In colonial America, you were apprenticed for six or more years to a master craftsman in order to learn the trade. You'd eat, drink, breathe, and work with that person to learn all that he had learned. Life knowledge was passed on in the context of a relationship, the opening up of one life to another. But the idea goes back even further than that—all the way back to the Bible. Jethro mentored his son-in-law, Moses. Moses then mentored his successor, Joshua. The prophet Elijah invested in the prophet Elisha. Mary, the mother of Jesus, turned to her older cousin, Elizabeth, for help. But one of the greatest models for mentoring can be found in the life of Jesus. He focused on 120 people, and from that, He singled out seventy for special training and attention. Then from the seventy, He poured Himself into twelve men—His intimate circle of disciples. He had those twelve men shadow His every step—eating with them, traveling with them, teaching them, living with them. And then, from among the twelve, three received particularly intensive time: Peter, James, and John. And He bet the farm on those men. He staked His entire mission and the future of the church on mentoring. Obviously, Jesus had a lot of confidence in the mentoring approach to spiritual development.

A good mentor will walk with you in life, be a true brother or sister, challenge your thinking and faith, caution you when appropriate, and share what he or she has learned that might help you. Today, it's easy to get knowledge—what's tough is to get *wisdom*. But wisdom is what you can get from another person's life through your relationship with him or her.[17]

So how do you enter into a mentoring relationship? Just keep your eye out for someone whom you respect, who seems strong in an area in which you would like to grow and with whom you seem to click. And then begin to develop that relationship and spend some time with that person. And in the course of that time, invest in learning all you can, asking questions and becoming something of a student of his or her life. I have a man in my life who is a mentor to me in regard to leadership. Another man is a mentor in the area of my spiritual life. For several years Susan and I had a married couple who mentored us in regard to our marriage. They had been married twenty-five years longer than we had, with five kids to our four. We would get together with them about every two months, and we would learn more on a single evening than we would have gained in a dozen books or a month of seminars.

Join a Small Group

A third step you can take is to become involved in some form of small group within the larger group of your community, such as a Sunday school class, home Bible study group, or serving team. Small groups can provide a powerful environment for spiritual growth. A small group is just that—a small group of people who get together to build relationships, study the Bible, and encourage each other in the faith. It provides extended periods of time to join with others to help apply biblical truth to real-life situations. It is a small community within the larger community, where you can experience the forgiveness and healing you want, along with the challenge, encouragement, and support you need. It's a set of Christian friends who can become a support group for your faith.

I can't begin to tell you how many times I've gone to the hospital to visit people and discovered that a long stream of people from their small group had already been by to see them, pray for them, arrange meals for them, and care for their needs. They didn't need me to come by; in fact, when I showed up, they wondered what I was doing there—maybe they had taken a turn for the worse and the doctors had called me in to break the news! A small group can become your personal community within the larger community, your network of relationships that feeds and strengthens your spiritual life. Your small group can become a group of people who know you, care about you, love you, and are committed to your spiritual growth and development. Without this "community within the community," you'll miss out on a level of support that those who have experienced couldn't *imagine* trying to survive without. They would liken it to trying to grow up in a home without a family.

A WORD TO THE RELATIONALLY CHALLENGED

I know that for many of you, relationships are difficult. Many of us have made the mistake of investing ourselves into relationships that have left us deeply wounded. We've been abandoned, taken advantage of, betrayed, or misunderstood; when that's happened, we felt like someone took a knife, plunged it into our hearts, and twisted it around a few times. I read of one father who wanted to teach his six-year-old daughter about the world, so he had her stand on the edge of her bed. He stood a couple of feet away and said, "Jump, honey; I'll catch you!" Hesitantly, the little girl gathered herself and leaped off the bed. When she did, her father moved back and let her fall to the floor. When she hit, she cried, "Why did you drop me, Daddy?"

115

"Because," said the father, "I want you to learn not to trust anyone."[18]

Sometimes it feels like we go from relationship to relationship, and the pain happens over and over again. So we just harden ourselves, lock up our hearts, and throw away the key. Nobody gets in, because when they do, it just means more pain. When we think back on the times we've experienced pain, we realize it's usually happened because of another person. And over time, we can shut the door and tighten down the hatches. We can develop an attitude that says, "I will not be hurt again." And then we begin to go through our lives emotionally detached. People can get close, but not too close. While that may keep us from being hurt by people, it doesn't keep us from hurting. The only pain worse than being hurt through a relationship is the pain of isolation and loneliness that comes from shutting yourself off from relationships.

I know. I am a very relationally challenged person. Intimacy has never been an easy affair. I grew up believing that it was best not to tell anyone anything you didn't have to, because nobody could be trusted; they would just use it against you down the road. I changed schools many times throughout my adolescence—following the first grade, second grade, third grade, sixth grade, seventh grade, eighth grade, ninth grade, and tenth grade. Added to that is the fact that I'm a borderline introvert: I gain my emotional energy from being alone. So if anyone knows the difficulties of making this investment, I do. I have to *constantly* work at it. But I am going to be in strategic relationships with people through mentoring and small groups for the rest of my life—not because it's easy for me, and not because I always want to, but because it's *critical* for the life I want to live—and it's critical for yours too.

No matter who you are or where you are, we need to do this *together.*

---

1. What person is a good example to you of how the Christian life should be lived?

2. Why are words of encouragement so helpful? When did you last feel encouraged by someone else?

3. Who is a VRP to you, who mentors you and ignites your love for God? What two or three friends are VIPs to you and share your same level of spirituality?

4. Where are you most susceptible to your VDPs, those who weaken and drain you?

5. What do you think would help strengthen your relationships?

CHAPTER SEVEN

How to Worship

As an American, I can admit that we are an odd people. We founded our country on the rejection of kings and monarchs, yet we watched the wedding of Princess Diana in rapt fascination and joined with the world in weeping tears at her death. We are fascinated by the lives, circumstances, ritual, and ceremony of the royal families in Europe, but we wouldn't tolerate one of *our* politicians putting on such airs for one minute. It's almost as if we don't want to have royalty over us politically, but we want there to be a sense of royalty somewhere in the world. We want something magical, mythical, and grand that we can look to in awe and wonder and—if we're honest—worship.

The word *worship* comes from an old Anglo-Saxon word that literally reads "worth-ship," and it means just that—to give worth or honor to someone or something. And we long to do that, whether through the innocence of hero worship or the bending of our hearts toward God. The actor Val Kilmer, commenting on his role as the voice of Moses in the film *Prince of Egypt*, spoke for many when he said, "It doesn't matter the genre. It doesn't matter the style. It doesn't matter the language. We want that sacred thing."[1] The reason is simple: We were *made* for worship, and our hearts are restless until they have found the object of worship that we were created to honor.

What Makes Worship So Important

Until you become a worshiper of the One who is worthy of worship, the One who created you, formed you, and called you into being, you will never experience the spiritual depth and vitality that you were designed for. In fact, of all the spiritual investments that can be made, this may be the deepest, most penetrating, personal, life-changing investment of all. Yet it may also be the one people understand the least—and certainly *do* the least. As Chuck Swindoll once put it, our tendency is to worship our work, work at our play, and play at our worship. But playing at worship will cause us to miss out on all that worship can bring to our lives, beginning with its role in helping us order our lives around God.

Worship Helps You Order Your Life around God

I read of a radio broadcaster who said that a man once wrote in to his station asking him to sound the musical note A on his morning show. The man said that he was a shepherd out on a remote ranch, far away from a piano. His only comfort was his old violin, and it was completely out of tune. The radio host agreed, sounded the note on his show, and then received a short note that simply read: "Thanks. Now I am in tune." A simple little story, but it reminds us what worship can be in our lives—a clear, solid note that allows us to retune our lives to God. Gathering with others to bring all of our energies and senses to bear on the honor of God brings our lives into alignment with the heart of our spirituality. As Richard Foster has noted, "If worship does not change us, it has not been worship."[2]

Worship Helps You Encounter and Experience God

A second reason worship is so vital to our spiritual lives is that it helps us encounter and experience God. No one wants dead, lifeless ritual. We don't want dried-out dogma. We don't want meaningless symbols and practices. We want to *engage* God, to *experience* God. And God wants that for us too. And He's designed the way for it to happen: worship. Jesus promised that "where two or three come together in my name, there am I with them" (Matt. 18:20). God is present in the gathered community of worship in a way unlike any other moment. And His presence is there for *encounter*.

Worship Helps You Respond to God

A third benefit of worship for your life is that it helps you respond to God. When you love someone, it's natural to want to let those feelings be known. You want to *tell* them, *show* them, *do something* for them—even though some of us are a bit out of practice.

I love the story of the guy who made a new commitment to demonstrate his love to his wife. He usually left his job sweating and dirty, so one day he cleaned up before he came home. He then stopped by a florist and bought a dozen red roses. Arriving at their front door, he rang the doorbell and waited for his wife to answer. When she opened the door, he proudly held out the flowers and said, "For you, honey! I love you!"

She looked at the flowers, looked at her husband, and then *burst into tears!* She cried, "I've had a terrible day! Billy broke his leg and I had to take him to the hospital. I no sooner got home from the hospital than the phone rang. It was your mother. She's coming to visit for two weeks. Then I tried to do all the laundry, and the washing machine broke, and now there's water all over the basement floor . . .

"*. . . and now you have come home drunk!*"[3]

Worship is one of the most personal, sincere, authentic ways to respond to God relationally. And when you articulate your feelings, expressing yourself verbally and emotionally and physically, it deepens your relationship with God. I can't imagine being in a growing, intimate relationship with my wife without regularly telling her how I feel about her, how much I care about her, that she's important to me, and that I love her. This is why the Bible presents worship in terms of expression, such as in the Seventy-first Psalm: "I will praise you with music, telling of your faithfulness to all your promises. . . . I will . . . sing your praises for redeeming me. I will talk to others all day long about your justice and your goodness" (vv. 22–24 TLB). And in Psalm 59, David, the king of Israel, said: "I will sing about your strength; every morning I will sing aloud of your constant love. You have been a refuge for me, a shelter in my time of trouble. I will praise you . . . the God who loves me" (vv. 16–17 TEV). I know that many people have a hard time expressing their feelings to other people, much less God. But even the most awkward attempts at expressing that love matter.

Worship Helps You Celebrate God

A fourth payoff is that worship helps you celebrate God. To celebrate God is to take time to remember all that He's done and say, "Yea, God!" It's like having a party in His honor. Take a look at the spirit of this through the Ninety-sixth Psalm in the Bible:

> Sing Yahweh a brand-new song! Earth and everyone in it, sing! Sing to Yahweh—worship Yahweh! . . . For Yahweh is great, and worth a thousand Hallelujahs. . . . Bravo, Yahweh, Bravo! Everyone join in the great shout: Encore! In awe before the beauty, in awe before the might. Bring gifts and celebrate . . . everyone worship! . . . Get out the message—Yahweh rules! . . . Let's hear it from Sky, with Earth joining in, and a huge round of applause from Sea. Let Wilderness turn cartwheels, animals, come dance, put every tree of the forest in the choir—an extravaganza before Yahweh as he comes. (MSG)

Now that's a party! And we need to take time to do that. We need to stop and applaud and cheer. As the supervisor of a large staff and an even larger team of volunteers, I've learned the importance of taking time to *celebrate.* If we don't hit the pause button in the midst of the push and pull of what we are trying to accomplish together to remember all that has been accomplished so far, then we can lose our passion and vision for the ongoing demands of the task. It's important to stop and say, "You know, it's been a good season. Let's just stop and have a party." But as important as that is organizationally, it is even more important *spiritually.*

The Bible says that every good and perfect gift is from God. Everything good, everything noble, everything praiseworthy, everything that has worth and merit and truth and goodness, is from Him. And what moves your spiritual life from one that is drab, lifeless, and boring to one that is exciting, high-energy, and just flat-out fun is to learn how to celebrate all of that! Worship is God's way of saying, "Loosen up a little and have some fun! You're *way* too uptight—life is meant to be a *celebration* of all that I am, all that I have done, and all that I am doing in you, with you, and through you." And when you add some of that to your spiritual life, it makes a world of difference.

Worship Helps You Receive Spiritual Encouragement and Energy

Finally, worship helps you receive spiritual encouragement and energy. You may recall the verses we looked at earlier from the Book of Hebrews: "Let us consider how we may spur one another on toward love and good deeds. Let us not give up meeting together, as some are in the habit of doing, but let us encourage one another" (10:24–25). While the primary purpose of worship is not what we get out of it, but what we give to God *through* it, when you gather together with others to worship, there's no way you can walk away without a good, solid dose of spiritual energy and encouragement.

I'll never forget traveling to Urbana, Illinois when I was in college for a huge gathering of university students sponsored by InterVarsity Christian Fellowship. InterVarsity is an outreach ministry to students that is based on college campuses around the world, and it was through InterVarsity that I began my relationship with Christ as a twenty-year-old sophomore in college. More than seventeen thousand of us crammed into an auditorium on the campus of the University of Illinois at Champaign-Urbana on New Year's Eve for a worship celebration. What we didn't know was that the top of the auditorium had become covered with huge sheets of ice. As we sang, pouring out our hearts in celebration of God, vibrations from our voices began to shake the ice loose. So as we were singing, we could hear huge sheets of ice sliding off the top of the auditorium, serving as a thunderous echo to our offering to God.

Joining voices with thousands of other people, hearing the rumble of ice coming off the building as we sang, and then, at midnight, taking communion together to usher in the new year, was simply one of the most remarkable shots of spiritual adrenaline I've ever experienced. That's the nature of worship.

How to Worship

So how do you do it? Is worship simply attending a service? Not according to Jesus. Here's what He had to say: "True worshipers will worship the Father in spirit and truth, for they are the kind of worshipers the Father seeks. God is spirit, and his worshipers must worship in spirit and in truth" (John 4:23–24). When it comes to worship, Jesus taught two things—that we should worship God in *spirit* and in *truth*. Let's start off with truth.

Worshiping God in Truth

To worship in truth means that when we worship God, we really worship God, as He *really is,* not some false idea of God or some substitute for God. True Christian worship rests not only on the *act* of worship, but on the *object* of worship. To worship in truth means to worship the only true object for worship—*God.* There are many other objects you could choose to worship—money, fame, a rock, a tree, even a distorted view of God—but that wouldn't be the worship you were created for, much less a worship that would do anything for your life. Because only worship in truth—the worship of the one, true God as revealed in Scripture—is really worship.

Worshiping God in Spirit

But that's not all that Jesus said. He also said to worship in spirit. To worship in spirit is to worship authentically with your *heart,* to have your act of worship be sincere, genuine, and real. Jesus said it's not just *whom* you worship that matters, but *how* you worship.

There's an old story about a man who went to church with an angel as his guide. Every seat in the sanctuary was filled, but there was something strange about the service. The organist moved her fingers over the keys, but no music came from its pipes. The choir rose to sing, and their lips moved, but not a sound was to be heard. The pastor stepped to the pulpit to read the Scriptures, but the man with the angel could not even detect the rustle of the pages. The Lord's Prayer was recited by the entire congregation, but not a single syllable was audible. The pastor again went to the pulpit, and the man watched as the minister gestured here and there to make his various points, but he heard nothing.

Turning to the angel, the man said, "I don't understand. What does all of this mean? I see that a service is being held, but I hear nothing."

The angel replied, "You hear nothing because there is nothing to be heard. You see the service as God sees it. These people honor Him with their lips, but their hearts are far from Him. Worship without the heart is not worship."

WAYS TO WORSHIP

So we are to worship in spirit and truth. That's easy enough to understand. But what are some of the ways of doing that?

Music

One of the most common, and most significant, ways to worship God is through music. There are forty-one different psalms in the Bible that encourage us to sing to God. There's something about music that moves us and lets us express ourselves in powerful and meaningful ways. To use music to worship God, we take the words to the song and make them *our* words. We use it as a vehicle to express how *we* feel and what *we* want to say. As the Hundredth Psalm says, "Sing yourselves into his presence" (v. 2 MSG).

Body

A second way you can worship is through your body. Look at this sampling of verses from the Bible:

"I lift up my hands toward your Most Holy Place" (Ps. 28:2).

"I spread out my hands to you" (Ps. 88:9).

"The people all stood up. . . . All the people lifted their hands and responded, 'Amen! Amen!' Then they bowed down and worshiped the LORD with their faces to the ground" (Neh. 8:5–6).

We are physical creatures, and we tend to express ourselves physically. What do you naturally do when you get excited at a football game? Let's say the quarterback of your favorite team connects to the tight end for a touchdown to win the game. Do you just sit there and yawn? No way! You go *nuts!* You jump up and cheer, clap and shout, slap your neighbor on the back, and pump your fist in the air. The more comfortable you get with worship, the more comfortable you become with expressing yourself physically to God in ways that seem natural and appropriate to who you are and how you're feeling. I don't mean you do an end-zone dance—when it comes to worship, you should never act in a way that draws attention to yourself—but when you worship, you might want to kneel, you might want to clap, you might want to close your eyes and just soak it all in, or you might want to raise your hand as a symbol of praise. Your body is part of who you are, and it is often essential to expressing yourself in worship to God.

Acts and Events

A third way we can worship is through certain acts and events. In the Bible, taking up an offering is considered an act of worship. Praying can be an act of worship. There are two acts of worship that deserve special attention. One is a solitary, one-time event, while the other is an ongoing investment. The single event is baptism, and the continued practice is the celebration of communion, also known as the Eucharist (a word for "thankfulness") or the Lord's Supper. Both are command performances for your spiritual life. Let's begin with baptism.

Christian Baptism

Jesus was baptized, and He taught that everyone who chooses to follow Him be baptized as well. In one of the most famous passages in the Bible, known as the Great Commission, Jesus said: "Go, then, to all peoples everywhere and make them my disciples: baptize them in the name of the Father, the Son, and the Holy Spirit, and teach them to obey everything I have commanded you" (Matt. 28:19–20 TEV). This makes baptism one of the clearest demonstrations that you really are a Christian. For the Bible says that "we know that we have come to know him if we obey his commands" (1 John 2:3).

So what is the meaning of baptism? First and foremost, it illustrates Christ's death, burial, and resurrection. The Bible says, "For when you were baptized, you were buried with Christ, and in baptism you were also raised with Christ" (Col. 2:12 TEV). Baptism also illustrates your new life as a Christian. Notice how this is expressed in the Bible: "By our baptism, then, we were buried with him and shared his death, in order that, just as Christ was raised from death . . . so also we might live a new life!" (Rom. 6:4 TEV). In fact, in the very early life of the ancient church, when people emerged from the baptismal waters, they would be clothed with a white robe to symbolize their new life in Christ, free from the stain of sin. Yet baptism doesn't make you a Christian. Only your faith in Christ does that. Baptism is like a wedding ring—it's the outward sign of the commitment you have made within your heart.

Most people know that there are differences in the way churches baptize people. Some do it by immersion, others by sprinkling. Most have concluded that immersion is most in line with the biblical evidence, not to mention the spirit of the symbol as it relates to Christ's burial and resurrection.[4] It seems to be the way Jesus Himself was baptized, and every other baptism recorded in the Bible was by immersion.[5] Also, the word *baptize* itself is a transliteration of the Greek word *baptizo,* which means to dip, plunge, or immerse under water.[6] But the *method* of baptism is not as important as the *act* of baptism. Every person who becomes a Christian should be baptized as a Christian. In the Bible, we find a close connection between decision and public profession of faith. For example, the Book of Acts records: "Those who believed . . . were baptized . . . that day!" (2:41 GN). And when Philip led an Ethiopian man to Christ, the eunuch said, "'Look, here is water. Why shouldn't I be baptized?' Philip said, 'If you believe with all your heart, you may.' The eunuch answered, 'I believe that Jesus Christ is the Son of God.' . . . Then both Philip and the eunuch went down into the water and Philip baptized him" (Acts 8:36–38). But this does not mean that baptism has to follow immediately after salvation. What the Bible is trying to teach is that baptism should follow your decision to become a believer. There is no reason to delay. If you wait until you are "good" enough, you will never feel ready for baptism.

If you were baptized as an infant, then it is likely your faith tradition has some form of confirmation process that should be followed with sincere conviction, else the purpose and meaning of your baptism has been lost. To quote Shakespeare, it was an event that, sadly, was "full of sound and fury, signifying nothing."[7] The purpose of baptism is to confess your personal commitment to Christ publicly; regardless of method, this purpose must not be lost. If you have not been baptized, or if an earlier event failed to represent a true declaration of faith, you will want to pursue Christian baptism.[8]

The Lord's Supper

The second act of worship commanded by Jesus was to remember His death through the taking of bread and wine. Unlike the once-for-all nature of Christian baptism, the Lord's Supper is to be repeated with great frequency in our lives as an active memorial.

The background for the Lord's Supper is the Jewish Passover festival, which marked how the Jewish people had been liberated from

Egyptian bondage through the plagues God brought on Egypt through Moses. The tenth and decisive plague was the death of the firstborn of Egypt.

The sacrifice of an animal was a common way for people of that culture to atone for their sins, and God told the Israelites that if they would sacrifice an unblemished lamb—one without a defect—and then take that blood and spread it on their doorposts, the angel of death would pass over them and not take the life of their firstborn; hence the term *Passover.*

People put the blood on the doorposts, the angel came, the firstborn of Egypt were killed, but the Israelites were passed over. This had such an impact on the leaders of Egypt that they released the Israelites from bondage, and Jewish people have been celebrating the festival of Passover ever since as a reminder of God's deliverance from death and the freedom that came from that deliverance through the blood of a lamb.

As the festival developed, it came to involve a lamb that would be slaughtered and eaten, along with unleavened bread as a symbol that their departure from Egypt was so hurried that they were unable to add yeast. Even more importantly, the bitter taste of the unleavened bread would remind them of the bitterness of the bondage from which they had been released. And then a cup of wine was always set aside for the Messiah, in case He came that very night to bring deliverance. The Passover was always to be celebrated as a family, to remind the Israelites that they were saved as a community and called out of bondage as a community, in order to be a community.[9]

Just before His death, Jesus gathered His disciples together to celebrate the Passover, but with a twist. He said that now this wine and bread was to have a new meaning. From now on, the meal would serve to represent *Him* as the unblemished lamb that was sacrificed. And those that would be marked by *His* blood would be freed from the bondage of their sin and would be passed over from the spiritual death that comes from sin.

Jesus said from now on, Christians should "do this in remembrance of me" (Luke 22:19). The Lord's Supper is the *new* memorial meal for those who are part of the family of God. The bread is eaten in remembrance of His body, broken for us. And the wine is a symbol of His blood shed on the cross. And the cup set aside for the Messiah is now raised to our lips—for the Messiah, in the person of Jesus, has come.

Jesus was the true sacrificial lamb for the Passover; His death would now serve as the ultimate and final deliverance of God's people from their sins. This is why Paul writes in his letter to the church at Corinth that "Christ, our Passover lamb, has been sacrificed" (1 Cor. 5:7). And the church has been celebrating the Lord's Supper ever since as a family of faith. The impact of this special act of worship cannot be measured. The Lord's Supper is a time of remembrance, but this is far from mere recollection in our memory. The Greek word Jesus used for *remembrance* is best understood as an affectionate calling of the person to mind, a reliving of a past event. Jesus wanted this meal to be a remembrance that would transport what was buried in the past to a dynamic place in the present. So through the celebration of the Supper we remember

Christ's death, our acceptance of His death on our behalf, our promise at baptism to lead a new life, and the spiritual strength and blessing that God has given—and will give us—for our spiritual journey. It is the high point of Christian worship.

FROM RUSSIA, WITH MEANING

I mentioned earlier that I visited Moscow in the spring of 1994 as a visiting professor at the Moscow Theological Institute. One night a group of us went to the famed Bolshoi Ballet. It was a long, wonderful evening, but after we took the subway back to where we were staying, the students said, "Come and let us celebrate." The other two professors with me were as tired as I was, but the students were so intent on our joining them that we went. And then we found out what celebration meant to them. They wanted to gather in the dining room and sing hymns of worship to God. And we did, late into the night, with more passion and sincerity than I have ever experienced. It didn't matter that we didn't sing in Russian—we worshiped God together.

But I went to bed puzzled. I had never seen such hearts for spontaneous and heart-filled worship. I was curious as to why they were so ready and eager to offer God love and honor. I received my answer the following Sunday when I was invited to speak at a church in North Moscow. A former underground church that met in secret, as so many churches had been, they were now meeting openly in a schoolhouse. I had been asked to bring a message that Sunday morning. I didn't know that I was in for a bit of a wait.

The service lasted for nearly three hours. There were three sermons from three different speakers, with long periods of worship between each message. And I was to go last. When it was over, I talked a bit with the pastor of the church. I was surprised at not only the length of the service, but the spirit and energy of the people. During the entire three hours, they never let up. Throughout the service, they never seemed to tire. Even at the end, they didn't seem to want to go home.

"In the States," I said, "you're doing well to go a single hour before every watch in the place starts beeping." He didn't get my weak attempt at humor, but he did say something that I will never forget.

"It was only a few years ago that we would have been put in prison for doing what we did today. We were never allowed to gather together as a community of faith and offer worship to God. And we are just so happy, and almost in a state of unbelief, that we can do this now—publicly, together—that we don't want it to end. And not knowing what the future might hold for us here, we assume that every week might just be our last. So we don't ever want to stop. So we keep worshiping together, as long as we can."

As I left, his words never left my mind. And I thought to myself, *I will never think about worship the same again. I've been too casual about it, too laid-back, taken it too much for granted. These people know what worship is really about and because of that, they have been willing, and would be willing again, to suffer for it. To be imprisoned for it. To die for it. They've discovered that true worship*

135

has a high yield for their lives. The simple act of worship has that much meaning and significance to them. It matters that much.

And then I thought, *And it should matter that much to me.*

---

1. What does it mean to worship God in truth?

2. How can a person worship God in spirit?

3. Each person has unique talents and different modes of expression. What form of worship comes easiest to you? (e.g., music, singing, giving, serving, praying, writing, etc.)

4. Since God accepts all kinds of worship—from a hard work ethic to showing patience with coworkers to even athletic competition—then how can someone begin to consider all of life as an act of worship?

CHAPTER EIGHT

Becoming a Player

When you were young, what did you want to be when you grew up? Several years ago, when my oldest daughter Rebecca was only four, she informed my wife that when she grew up, she was going to be a farmer.

My wife said, "That's nice, dear."

"Yep," Rebecca continued, "when I grow up, I'm gonna be a farmer, and I'm gonna marry Daddy!"

Then Susan said, "But if you grow up and become a farmer and marry Daddy, what will *Mommy* do?"

Rebecca pondered that seriously for a moment or two, then she brightened up and said, "You can be our cow!"

All of us have different dreams, different ideas of what we want our lives to be like. And for most of us, there is a common denominator: *We want to make a difference.* We want our lives to stand out and to count for something. We know we are players in a game, and we don't want to be sitting on the bench.

WHY IS SERVING OTHERS IMPORTANT?

Making a difference matters—not just in terms of personal fulfillment, but in regard to spiritual development. And the heart of difference making is the giving away of yourself, the investing of yourself. According to the math of spirituality, the more you give, the more you receive. This is why Jesus was simultaneously the most influential figure in all of human history and the ultimate model of spiritual living. For He "did not come to be served, but to serve," and to give His life away (Mark 10:45).

So how does this actually work? In four ways:

Serving Others Gets You into Spiritual Shape

First, serving others gets you into spiritual shape. It's how you get a spiritual workout. When you serve, you build up your faith. Think about how it works with your body. When you lift weights, you increase the levels of contractile proteins and connective tissue in the muscles you exercise, making those muscles bigger than they were before. Your spiritual life works that way when it comes to serving, because it is through serving that you give your faith the necessary workout it needs to grow strong. If you're *not* serving, your spiritual life will be weak, flabby, and undeveloped.

Serving Others Gets You into the Game

A second payoff is that serving others gets you into the game. It's the way you become a player and get involved in what God is doing in the world. This is one of our chief purposes in life, for the

Bible says: "God has made us what we are. He has created us in Christ Jesus to live lives filled with good works that he has prepared for us to do" (Eph. 2:10 GW). You were created to take who God made you to be and put yourself into play. And following that purpose will put more gas into your spiritual tank than you could possibly imagine. Think about it: Are you more passionate about something you're involved in or something you just watch from a distance? When you get off the sidelines and become a player for God, what God is doing becomes a lot more important to you.

Serving Others Lets You Make a Difference

The third payoff of serving others is one we've already explored: It enables you to make a difference in this world, to do something more than just making money, or putting together a business deal, or buying a dream house, or taking a vacation. We want our lives to count; we want to do something with our lives that will matter. And there's only one way for that to happen: to make the investment of service. And once you do, make no mistake, you will taste what making a difference is all about. All you have to do is see one changed life, hear one thank-you, see one brief glimpse of impact from some act of service that you've done, and your life will never be the same. Then you'll see things from a different vantage point—a little higher, a little more eternal. And you'll say, "Most of the stuff I've done with my life won't add up to much, but this, this will live on; this mattered; this made a difference." And it doesn't get much better than that.

Serving Others Amplifies Your Impact

Throughout his presidency of the United States, Ronald Reagan kept a sign on his desk that said, "It's amazing how much you can get done if you don't care who gets the credit." Making a difference does not always mean taking center stage. Serving enables something to take place because you supported it and helped make it happen. Leonard Bernstein, the famous orchestra conductor, performed one evening on television. During an informal time of discussion on the program, an admirer asked: "Mr. Bernstein, what is the most difficult instrument to play?" He responded quickly: "Second fiddle. I can get plenty of first violinists, but to find one who plays *second* violin with as much enthusiasm or *second* French horn or *second* flute, now that's a problem. And yet if no one plays second, we have no harmony."[1] True servanthood is what allows you to make a strategic difference.

But this life of service to others is a high calling. Consider the following words by Ruth Harms Calkins:

> *You know, Lord, how I serve You*
> *With great emotional fervor*
> *In the limelight.*
> *You know how eagerly I speak for You*
> *At a women's club.*
> *You know how I effervesce when I promote*
> *A fellowship group.*
> *You know my genuine enthusiasm*
> *At a Bible study.*

But how would I react, I wonder
If You pointed to a basin of water
And asked me to wash the calloused feet
Of a bent and wrinkled old woman
Day afer day
Month after month
In a room where nobody saw
And nobody knew.[2]

One of the most influential, high-impact men I know serves on the staff of our church as a volunteer. Lloyd bought and sold his first piece of property at the age of fourteen. By his early thirties, he had become a millionaire. But God tapped him on the shoulder of his heart and raised a single question: "How much is enough?"

The question plagued Lloyd and led to an extraordinary set of life choices. He restructured his holdings in such a way that they would generate a modest salary through which he and his family could live for the rest of their adult lives. He then removed himself from the day-in, day-out world of business and devoted his life to full-time Christian service. God has used his expertise and leadership in the life of our church and in the life and direction of other organizations around the nation, in ways that few will ever know, see, or appreciate. He's formulated strategic plans, stimulated evangelistic awareness, and challenged others in the marketplace to give their lives more fully to Christ. Few will ever know Lloyd's name, but without him, there would be less harmony in the world.

DISCOVER YOUR PLACE

So how do you "develop your serve" and become a player for God? It begins by discovering your *place.* Thomas Merton wrote that "a tree gives glory to God by being a tree."[3] He also wrote that "each particular being, in its individuality . . . with all its own characteristics and its private qualities and its own inviolable identity, gives glory to God by being precisely what He wants it to be here and now, in the circumstances ordained for it."[4] The beginning move for anyone is to discover their place of service in light of who God made them to be. That involves five major areas to explore, beginning with *passion.*

Passion

If I were to take a random survey and ask people what the word *passionate* means, the top answer would undoubtedly relate to romance. But that's not the only meaning of the term. In fact, the dictionary defines *passion* as "intense emotional drive . . . burning intensity . . . zeal . . . enthusiasm."[5] Most of us have certain things that we are passionate about, certain topics or activities that we care about on a deep, even emotional level. When we think about these things, we become energized. When we do anything related to it, we get pumped up. Our eyes light up when we talk about it. It's a *passion!* Now some passions are superficial. It's no secret among those who know me that I am passionate about basketball. But basketball is not a deep passion, something that could fill the very purpose of my life. God's place for you will involve your deepest emotional heartbeat. That's why the Bible says to "watch over your heart; that's where life starts" (Prov. 4:23 MSG).

Natural Talents and Abilities

A second area to consider is your natural talents and abilities. The Bible says that "God has given each of us the ability to do certain things well" (Rom. 12:6 TLB). I can look at my children right now and tell you what at least some of their natural gifts and abilities are. At ages twelve, ten, eight, and six, it's already becoming clear. Rebecca, at twelve, has abilities in literature and creative writing. Rachel has natural strengths in the arts. My oldest son, Jonathan, is a natural athlete with strong people skills. My six-year-old son, Zachary, is clearly marked for professional sumo wrestling.

Most of us have areas where, at some point or another, it became clear we had natural ability and talent. That wasn't by chance! Unfortunately, these God-given strengths can become lost or overlooked for all the wrong reasons. A schoolteacher once told a seven-year-old boy he should drop out of school because he wasn't creative. That boy was Thomas Edison, who invented, among many other things, the light bulb, the telephone, and the phonograph. Someone else told Mozart that his music had too many notes, and no one would ever like it. Another told Rembrandt that his paintings would never be remembered. Another boy was told he was a poor student, especially in mathematics. Diagnosed as mentally slow, there was an effort to remove him from school. Good thing they let Einstein stay. The author of

Gone with the Wind was rejected by major publishers for years. The Decca recording company told the Beatles they didn't like their sound, because groups with guitars were on their way out. Walt Disney's first job was at a newspaper, and the editor told him he had—get this—no creativity.[6]

I came across an interesting little story that originated from a school newsletter:

Once upon a time, the animals decided they should do something meaningful to meet the problems of the new world. So they organized a school.

They adopted an activity curriculum of running, climbing, swimming and flying. To make it easier to administer the curriculum, all the animals took all the subjects.

The *duck* was excellent in swimming; in fact, better than his instructor. But he made only passing grades in flying, and was very poor in running. Since he was slow in running, he had to drop swimming and stay after school to practice running. This caused his web feet to be badly worn, so that he was only average in swimming. But average was quite acceptable, so nobody worried about that—except the duck.

The *rabbit* started at the top of his class in running, but developed a nervous twitch in his leg muscles because of so much make-up work in swimming.

The *squirrel* was excellent in climbing, but he encountered constant frustration in flying class because his teacher made him start from the ground up instead of from the treetop down. He developed "charlie horses" from overexertion, and so only got a C in climbing and a D in running.

The *eagle* was a problem child and was severely disciplined for being a non-conformist. In climbing classes he beat all the others to the top of the tree, but insisted on using his own way to get there.[7]

Take an inventory of your life. Were you a natural leader as a child, but now you're in a situation where that skill isn't being used at all? Were you once attracted to the arts but haven't involved yourself in them for years? Did you once love to write, but for whatever reason, you stopped writing? Go back over your life, and take note of natural strengths, natural talents, and natural abilities. These abilities aren't just "natural"—they are *super*natural because of Who made you.

Personality

A third area to explore in order to direct your life toward making a difference as a servant has to do with your personality. The Bible says, "[God] created my inmost being; you knit me together in my mother's womb. . . . I am fearfully and wonderfully made" (Ps. 139:13–14). God created everything about you—even your *inmost being.* There is little doubt that each of us has a specific, unique personality. Some of us have personalities that are more unique than *others,* but we'll leave that alone. Regardless of your personality type, it was given to you by God. Some of us are extroverts; others are introverts. Some are thinkers; others are feelers.

Some of us are organized; others of us are, well, *not*. The Bible says in 1 Corinthians that "God works through different men in different ways" (12:6 PHILLIPS). Part of discovering your place of impact will involve your personality, because every personality has its own set of strengths and weaknesses, making some areas of service and investment better than others. I am a borderline introvert. This often surprises people, because the caricature of an introvert is someone who is quiet, shy, mild-mannered, and behind-the-scenes. I am none of those things. But I manifest one of the classic *marks* of introversion—namely, that I draw my emotional energy from being alone, and constant relational interchange can be terribly taxing on my body and soul. Knowing this has greatly impacted the *how, when, what,* and *where* of my service.

Past Experiences

A fourth area that is worth exploring is your past experiences. In Romans, the Bible says, "We know that all that happens to us is working for our good if we love God and are fitting into his plans" (8:28 TLB). Each one of us has a unique set of life experiences. Those experiences have given us an incredible amount of knowledge, experience, and wisdom. We have each had certain educational experiences, vocational experiences, and spiritual or ministry experiences that have left us with something of a deposit in our life accounts. The Bible says that those experiences were probably deposited in your account for a reason. Even the painful ones.

On May 3, 1980, Clarence William Busch killed thirteen-year-old Cari Lightner in a hit-and-run accident in Fair Oaks, California. Just two days earlier, Busch had been released on bail for a drunk-driving charge. His arrest for killing little Cari was his fourth drunk-driving arrest. Busch plea-bargained to a vehicular manslaughter charge. On November 25, 1980, the judge sentenced him to two years' imprisonment, which was less than the maximum three-year sentence. Busch never went to prison. He served his sentence in a work camp and a halfway house. In ten months, he was eligible to regain his driver's license. Outraged, Candy Lightner, the mother of the little girl Busch had killed, started the now-famous organization MADD—Mothers Against Drunk Driving. Today MADD has more than a million members and supporters in more than four hundred chapters in the United States, Canada, Australia, Great Britain, and New Zealand.

All from the death of her daughter.

Spiritual Gifts

Finally, but in many ways *most importantly,* there is the matter of your spiritual gifts. The Bible teaches a simple but important truth: Everyone who becomes a Christian receives the indwelling presence of the Holy Spirit. And when that happens, the Holy Spirit gives you, as a Christian, at least one spiritual gift to be used for what God is doing in this world through His church. Now what is a spiritual gift? Here's the simplest definition I know: A spiritual gift is a supernatural *ability* to develop a particular *capability* for making a difference with your life through serving.[8] The Bible says that "Christ has given each of us special abilities—whatever he wants us to have out of his rich storehouse of gifts" (Eph. 4:7 TLB). Not everyone has the same spiritual gift, and no one gift is better than another. But whatever your gift is, it's special, for it was expressly *given* to you by God

147

Himself. In J. R. R. Tolkien's *The Hobbit,* Gandalf the wizard told the reluctant and unlikely hero Bilbo, "There is more to you than you know." He said this knowing that Bilbo not only carried the blood from the more sedate Baggins side of the family, but also from the swashbuckling Took side. We, too, have more to us than we know—a mixture of the human and the divine—and one of the ways this manifests itself is through our spiritual gifts.[9]

Now you're probably wondering what kinds of gifts we're talking about. You will be familiar with most of them. There are speaking gifts, such as preaching and teaching; people gifts, such as counseling, encouragement, evangelism, hospitality, leadership, and mercy; and service gifts, such as administration, giving, and helps. The lists in the Bible are probably more suggestive than exhaustive, which means that the number and types of gifts are unlimited. What makes them *spiritual* gifts, though, and not just natural talents, is that these particular abilities are given to you by God when you become a Christian; if you will use them for service, God will *supernaturally empower* them for *maximum impact.* If you have never explored this aspect of your spiritual life, increasing numbers of churches are offering classes and seminars to help people discover their spiritual gifts.[10]

DEVELOP YOURSELF

The second step in becoming a player is to then take your passions, personality, abilities, experiences, and giftedness, and develop them as a package for service. Particularly your spiritual gift. It's a mistake to think that a spiritual gift is something you are able to *instantly* do *extraordinarily* well without practice and experience. Remember—a spiritual gift is not an instant ability, but a God-given capacity to *develop* an ability. For example, just because you have the spiritual gift of teaching doesn't mean that you are automatically a good communicator. Your gift may be teaching, but if you have no experience or training in teaching, you are probably an average teacher—even with the spiritual gift of teaching! There may be signs that God has enabled you in that area, but what you have is a supernatural capacity to *develop* the supernatural ability to teach. In a letter to a man he was mentoring by the name of Timothy, the apostle Paul said: "Do not neglect your gift. . . . Be diligent in these matters; give yourself wholly to them, so that everyone may see your progress" (1 Tim. 4:14–15). If you're a Christian, God has given you a spiritual gift, but you have to develop it.

GET IN THE GAME

This leads us to a third step. After you discover your place and begin developing your gifts and abilities, you must get in the game! The goal is to serve in light of all that you are, with all you are, in the context of the ministry of the church, and for the cause of Christ. And in all truth, this is how you best fulfill the second step, for the best development is in the course of actual practice. So don't let "time for development" keep you on the sidelines. The Bible says, "Offer yourselves as a living sacrifice to God, dedicated to his service" (Rom. 12:1 TEV). And then in verse 6 of that same chapter, it says, "So we are to use our different gifts" (TEV). And in Colossians, the Bible says, "Take heed to the ministry which you have received in the Lord, that you may fulfill it" (Col. 4:17 NKJV). And in 1 Peter, the Bible says, "God has given each of you some special abilities; be sure to use them" (4:10 TLB).

Do you see a theme there?

To discover your gift and get in touch with who you are is great, but it isn't enough. To develop yourself is wonderful, but it isn't enough. The goal is to put yourself into play! And when you do that, you will reach a level of spiritual fulfillment, energy, and passion that you can't experience any other way. There's an increase in spiritual vitality and fulfillment that can only come when you use your God-given, supernaturally empowered gift in ministry.

Now, let me anticipate what you might be thinking. This all sounds great to you—in fact, you get excited thinking about discovering your gifts, finding out where God might want you to invest yourself, and experiencing the thrill of making a difference. You have little doubt that serving others would serve your spiritual life well. But you're wondering how you're going to find the *time* to add *one more thing* to your already crowded, overflowing life. Fair enough. And I understand. But let me share a couple of time-related truths that I've learned.

First, we all tend to automatically fill our schedules. I can take someone's Day-Timer and remove every small group meeting, every ministry involvement, every midweek and weekend service, liberating those hours from that person's life. But you know what? In six weeks, he or she will just fill the schedule with something else. It's as if we can't stand a gap in time.

This leads to a second truth. We can fill our time with things that don't really matter, creating a life too full for what *is* important.

Most of us make "To Do" lists, but I once heard a speaker comment that what we really need are "Stop Doing" lists. We tend to be time spenders, not time investors. You can spend your life engaged in a number of activities; however, when you are at the end of your years, you'll look back and see that your life didn't add up to very much. You were busy, you were active, but yours wasn't a life of significance. If you invest your life, however, you have given your life to something you believe in, something bigger than yourself. Many people are heavily spent, and they're very, very busy. They're stretched to the limit. But they are not investing in anything.[11]

There comes a time when you say to yourself, *What do I want my life to be like? What am I going to prioritize?* The problem for many of us isn't a lack of time, but how we're choosing to *spend* our time. Scott Peck, a psychiatrist whom many know from his best-selling book *The Road Less Traveled,* once told an interesting story. There was a young Christian woman who lacked any semblance of joy in her life. She suffered from acute depression and was failing to respond to any form of therapy or treatment. Ready to give up on her, Peck was surprised one day to find her bouncing into his office full of joy and excitement. Asking her what was making her feel so good, she said that she was unable to get her car started that morning, so she called a minister friend and asked him if he could drive her to her appointment. He said he would, but on the way he had to stop by the hospital and make a few visits. She went with him and while he was in the hospital, she visited some elderly people in one of the wards. She read from the Bible and prayed with them. By the time the morning was over, she had never felt better. The emotional uplift was unmistakable. She hadn't felt that good in years.

Instantly, Peck recognized that this woman was benefiting from the investment of serving in an area of giftedness and passion. Peck then pointed out the good news, that they had found the way to make her happy and keep her out of depression. Then, much to his surprise, the woman responded, "You don't expect me to do this sort of thing every day, do you?"[12]

Developing your spiritual life through the practice of servant-hood does not start with your needs, but the needs of others. It does not begin with your schedule, but with what your schedule must *be* in *order* to serve. We are all busy, and we all have competing time demands. The question is whether we will order our lives around what it will take to experience a spiritual life or marginalize the pursuit of spirituality, where that pursuit will die the death of insignificance and inattention.

---

1. "God's place for you will involve your deepest emotional heartbeat" (page 142). What does that mean to you?

2. What are your natural talents and abilities, including those that have been lying dormant for years?

3. Thinking through your past experiences, what special experiences do you remember that will help you encourage or counsel others?

4. How can a person discover his or her spiritual gifts? What are yours?

CHAPTER NINE

Positioning Your Heart

This is a chapter about money. No games, no beating around the bush. And your spiritual life *needs* this chapter—as does mine—because money is more involved with our spirituality than any other single issue. Sound a bit over the top? Consider this: Two out of every three stories Jesus told had to do with money. More is said in the New Testament about money than about heaven and hell *combined.* Money is talked about in the Bible five times as often as prayer! In fact, there are more than *two thousand verses* in the Bible that deal with money.

Now you could be cynical and say that the reason for this emphasis is because all religions are money-oriented. I heard a joke about a guy who was on an airplane during a severe thunderstorm. The plane was suddenly struck by lightning, and they were forced to begin an emergency landing. A young woman turned to him and began screaming for him to do something *religious.* So he did the first religious thing that came to his mind. He took up an offering.[1]

I read about another guy who phoned a church and asked if he could speak with the "head hog at the trough."

The secretary said, "Who?"

The man repeated, "I want to speak to the head hog at the trough!"

The secretary said, "Sir, if you mean our pastor, you will have to refer to him with more respect."

"Oh, I see," said the man. "Well, all I wanted was to talk to him about this ten thousand–dollar gift I wanted to make to the church."

Then the secretary said, "Hold on—I think the big pig just walked in the door."[2]

But a less cynical and more knowledgeable view is that the reason there's so much in the Bible about money is because God knows how much your relationship with money reveals your heart and character—and not just reveals it, but *directs* it. So what I want to do is introduce you to God's *foundational principle* for money management, the one, single principle that is first and foremost in making sure your money serves your spiritual life instead of sabotages your spiritual life. And then from that, we'll look at four specific activities the Bible prescribes for us from that one foundational principle.

GOD'S FOUNDATIONAL FINANCIAL PRINCIPLE

The foundational spiritual principle related to money is this: God is the owner of it all, and we are the managers. The Bible says: "You may say to yourself, 'My power and the strength of my hands have produced this wealth for me.' But remember the LORD your God, for it is he who gives you the ability to produce wealth" (Deut. 8:17–18).

This principle carries with it some very important implications: First, if God owns it all, then He has all of the *rights* to what He owns. And since I only have what has been given to me, what I've been *allowed* to have, then I operate primarily in the realm of *responsibilities*.[3] That means that when it comes to money, there is a trust relationship between me and God. God has trusted me with certain resources that, in truth, He owns and has rights to. My job is to live by that trust by managing it well, according to His design and desire. He trusts me to do it.

A second implication is that if God owns it all, and I am someone who has simply been given the responsibility to manage those resources in a way that honors Him—then *every financial decision is a spiritual decision.* Whether it's buying a car, taking a vacation, investing in a mutual fund, paying taxes, or buying groceries— every spending decision is a spiritual decision, because I am managing the resources God has *given* me to manage. God cannot be shut out of any transaction, excluded from any purchase, omitted from any decision, or removed from any investment. It is, after all, His money. A final implication is that we are all accountable to God for this management. If all the money is His, and we are the managers of what He's allowed us to have, then ultimately we are accountable to Him for our money management. We'll all stand before a holy God one day and give an accounting for how we did with what He gave.

Now with that foundational principle in mind, we can walk through some of God's other principles, the specific instructions God has given to us about what He wants us to do with His money and what's best for us to do with it—because all of His principles are birthed in His love and care for us.

Give Back to God

First, God says to give. And not just in any way, to any place, but we are to give 10 percent of all that we've been allowed to earn to our local church. We can give more to our church or to other people or organizations if we like, but it starts with giving 10 percent to our church.

The prophet Malachi records these words from God to His people: "'Will a man rob God? Surely not! And yet you have robbed me.' 'What do you mean? When did we ever rob you?' 'You have robbed me of the tithes and offerings due to me. . . . Bring all the tithes into the storehouse'" (Mal. 3:8, 10 TLB).

That's a pretty clear word. And in Matthew, the Bible records Jesus plainly saying, "Yes, you should tithe" (23:23 TLB). The amount is not as important as the actual proportion or percentage. From this basis, the apostle Paul gave the following instruction to Christians in regard to the tithe and their local church: "Now here are the directions about . . . money. . . . On every Lord's Day each of you should put aside something from what you have earned during the week, and use it for [the] offering. The amount depends on how much the Lord has helped you earn" (1 Cor. 16:1–2 TLB).

As strong as this principle is, giving was never meant to be a legalistic, forced practice. That would ruin it as a *heart* issue. This is why the apostle Paul wrote the following words: "I want each of you to take plenty of time to think it over, and make up your own mind what you will give. That will protect you against sob stories and arm-twisting. God loves it when the giver delights in the giving" (2 Cor. 9:7 MSG). The motivation to give should never be guilt or pressure. It should never be fear or shame. Giving should be a matter of trust and obedience, love and commitment.

Why does God ask us to give? What is the spiritual significance of giving? The Bible suggests several reasons, but I'll just discuss four. First, we are asked to give because it is a clear reminder of who is the *owner* and who is the *manager*. Giving a full tithe is a clear declaration about whom our money *really* belongs to. It's the most tangible, direct indicator as to whether or not you are serious about your relationship with God.

A second reason God wants us to give is because it puts us in a relationship of dependence and trust. It *demands* faith. Giving back 10 percent of what He has given is not easy. If you're like me, you can think of all kinds of ways that money could be well spent toward items of security and comfort. Good things—responsible things. God knows that, but He wants us to look to Him for care. He wants us to see Him as trustworthy, as our Provider, as the One who will meet our every need. And that brings up something very important. Not only does the Bible teach us to tithe, but in the Bible we find that God promises to bless us in return. Look again at what God said through the prophet Malachi. After challenging the people on giving, God said: "If you do [tithe], I will open up the windows of heaven for you and pour out a blessing so great you won't have room enough to take it in! Try it! Let me prove it to you!" (Mal. 3:10 TLB).

Interestingly, this is the only place in the entire Bible where God ever said to test Him about anything—and it was in relation to finances. *Tithe,* He said, and *see* if I won't bless you. Jesus echoed this idea, saying, "Give to others, and God will give to you. Indeed, you will receive a full measure, a generous helping, poured into your hands—all that you can hold. The measure you use for others is the one that God will use for you" (Luke 6:38 TEV).

Here's what God offers: If you will manage your money in this way—giving 10 percent to your local church from all that you earn—then God promises to become supernaturally involved in your financial picture. If not, you're on your own. But if you'll trust Him, He's on board. And God says, "It'll be worth it. You'll be glad you did. Try Me." Now that doesn't mean you can tithe and then be irresponsible in every other area of your financial management, expecting God to continually bail you out. God has an entire set of principles that are important to follow that *never* call for financial irresponsibility. What God is saying is that He has a special blessing tied to people who do tithe, because no other action so clearly demonstrates allegiance to and orientation around the foundational principle that He's the owner and you're the manager. What God wants to demonstrate to each of us is that no matter how much we give, we'll never outgive *Him.* Following His principles will always bring more to our lives than we will ever lose.

The third reason God calls us to give holds enormous implication for our spiritual lives: Giving positions your heart. Look at this record of one of the most provocative things Jesus ever said: "Don't store up treasures on earth! Moths and rust can destroy them, and thieves can break in and steal them. Instead, store up your treasures in heaven, where moths and rust cannot destroy them, and thieves cannot break in and steal them. Your heart will always be where your treasure is" (Matt. 6:19–21 CEV).

Jesus is right. Where we have our money is where our interest lies—where we have a sense of ownership, a sense of investment. If there were a banking crisis, I would be most concerned about *my* bank. When I pick up the newspaper or hear a financial report on CNN, I care about *my* stocks, *my* mutual fund. That's just the way money works—it directs our attention and energies. Where your treasure is, there your heart will be—which is why giving to God puts your heart with *Him*. When you are investing in the kingdom of God, you become more interested in the kingdom of God. It grows in value and importance to you. It becomes essential to your focus and interest.

But giving goes deeper than that. It not only *directs* your heart; it should *reflect* your heart. It demonstrates that a real relationship is operating, that there really is a love functioning. Some years ago, when Susan and I celebrated our tenth wedding anniversary, I knew exactly what I wanted to give her. On our honeymoon, we had traveled to Colonial Williamsburg in Virginia. Every year on our anniversary we have gone back, even if it was just for a day or two. It's a very special place for us.

Susan's mom gave her a rather expensive charm bracelet for Christmas one year, and Susan had started collecting charms for it, ones that represented things of deep significance. One charm, a Christmas tree, was given to her by my mother, representing all of our Christmas Eves together. Another is a kiwi, for a long trip we took together to New Zealand. She is now collecting charms for each of our children. For our tenth anniversary, I wanted to give Susan a charm from Williamsburg, a golden pineapple, which is the colonial symbol for hospitality, love, and friendship. She had seen it on an earlier trip, and of all the charms that represented Williamsburg, that's the one she liked the best. I went to all kinds of trouble to get it for her without her knowing about it. And when I gave that to Susan, it meant the world to her—but it also meant the world to me. Not because of what it cost, not because of the trouble I went through to get it, but because of what it *meant*. It was a tie between us. I gave because it was a reflection of my heart.

One of my favorite Christmas stories is O. Henry's *The Gift of the Magi,* the tale of a very poor but hardworking man and his wife. As Christmas approaches, they realize that they have no money to buy each other even one gift. The man decides to sell his watch, one that had belonged to his father. It is his one prized possession, the one thing in his world of poverty for which he can be proud. But the love he has for his wife is greater than the love he has for his watch, so he sells it in order to buy a pair of combs for her long, lovely hair.

His wife is facing the same dilemma. She had been scrimping and saving for months for his Christmas present but had only managed a dollar or two. She sees an ad from a wig company that offers to pay money for human hair. Though she loves her hair very much, and it is the one thing in *her* world of poverty for which *she* can be proud, her love for her husband is much greater, so she sells her hair in order to buy a chain—*for his watch.*

Christmas Eve comes, and the man arrives at his house with his costly gift of hair combs for his wife—only to find she has no hair! She produces the beautiful chain for his watch—only to find *he* has no watch! They suddenly realize that while he can't use the chain and she can't use the combs—it doesn't matter. What mattered was the depth of the giving itself, which is why the play is called *The Gift of the Magi.* The title is taken from the wise men (magi) who visited the Christ child and wanted to give a gift to represent their love.

The final reason why God wants you to give is because when you do, it lets you experience the thrill of making a difference. There is no greater joy than witnessing and experiencing God working through what you give. It's fun to get statements from your mutual funds or your 401k and see what has been generated as a result of what you have put in. But that's nothing compared to the return you get when you give to what God is doing in the world.

At the church I pastor, I often tell folks that when they give, it matters. They are providing for little boys and little girls to hear that God is their friend and that He loves them. They are enabling people throughout the city to gather together in small groups in order to build relationships, grow closer to God, and enter into real, authentic community with each other. They are freeing up men and women to follow the call of God to come on staff in order to serve Him through full-time vocational ministry. They are bringing together middle-school and high-school students from a radically secular and postmodern culture to learn of the transforming power of God. They are allowing creative weekend services to be formed and presented that reach out to their friends with the message of Christ. I can point them to buildings and ministries, not to mention people with faces and names, families, and eternities that have been forever impacted through their giving. Show me a fund with that kind of return or any other financial statement that has that kind of payoff.

Avoid Unnecessary Debt

A second money-management principle is to avoid unnecessary and unhealthy debt.

When my wife and I first got married, we were like most young couples—*poor*. We didn't have any financial problems because we didn't have any finances to have problems *with*. But just a few months after we got married, I received a letter in the mail with "DO NOT FORWARD" in large letters on the outside. I opened it up, and out dropped my very own credit card with a thousand-dollar credit limit.

I couldn't believe it!

As far as we were concerned, somebody just handed us a check for a thousand dollars! Our minds became instantly filled with all kinds of things we hadn't been able to afford and were living comfortably without but now felt *strongly compelled* to purchase as an *absolute need*. So we went out and, before we knew it, had charged up seven or eight hundred dollars' worth of stuff. And we only had to make a payment of thirty or forty dollars a month. We could handle that. But as we were shopping around with our new card, we discovered that a lot of the major department stores had credit cards too. In fact, they advertised that if you had a credit card like ours, you could have a credit card for *their* store. And we thought, *God bless America*. So we went into one of those stores and plopped down our card and were promptly rewarded with five hundred dollars' worth of instant credit. And it just so happened that store was having a sale on really good stuff that we suddenly realized that we had always needed. The department store folks said the payments were only about fifteen or twenty dollars a month—so we thought, *No big deal!* We could always manage to scrape up that much.

Within a matter of weeks we had used up the limit on our credit card and the limit on our department store card. But by that time, we were hooked. We got card after card from store after store. With every purchase, we thought to ourselves, *What's another fifteen dollars a month?* Within a few months, we were in a financial mess, and we didn't have a clue how to get out of it. It got to the point that we were getting cash advances on our credit cards to pay our credit card bills! It took us years to dig ourselves out of a mess that only took a few months as newlyweds to create.

The Bible does not say that debt is a sin. It discourages the *use* of debt, but it doesn't *prohibit* debt. When it comes to debt, the Bible puts up a warning sign: "Danger Ahead."[4] And the danger of debt is that it often works *against* you rather than *for* you, and not just in terms of financial returns and interest rates. Debt limits you, costs you, even owns you. The Bible says, "The borrower is servant to the lender" (Prov. 22:7). As a pastor who works with the intricacies and intimacies of people's lives on a daily basis, I am convinced that the most binding, limiting, confining aspect of most people's lives is the debt they carry. Debt dictates, debt determines, and as a result, debt *enslaves*. In fact, it's one of the main reasons why people don't follow the principle of giving. Make no mistake—debt is a significant spiritual issue. Now we don't want to misunderstand the Bible on this one. We all know that there are some times that some debt is not only necessary, but strategic—particularly when you are talking about things such as houses, land, buildings, or something that appreciates in value over time. But one of God's most important money-management principles is to walk very carefully here. And if you've ever abused debt, like I have, you know why.

Save for the Future

A third money-management principle that God would have us follow is to be intentional about saving for the future. Nowhere does the Bible teach that we should presume upon the future. We don't know whether we'll keep making what we're making or keep working where we're working. God calls us to prepare for the unexpected by saving. As Proverbs 21 puts it, "The wise man saves for the future, but the foolish man spends whatever he gets" (v. 20 TLB). And even a small amount, regularly saved, will pay off with huge dividends. If you invest just $1.74 a day, which is about $52 a month, at a growth rate of 10 percent, in just two years you'd have over $1,300. In ten years, you'd have more than $10,000. And in forty years, you'd have more than $300,000. And that's at $1.74 a day.[5]

Live within Your Means

A final money-management principle, one that draws everything together and will allow you to take significant steps toward spiritual health and wholeness, is to live within your means. This includes developing a healthy budget based on God's principles and then following it. To do this, you start with what you make, subtract what it takes to honor God with a full tithe and cover your taxes, and then let the balance determine what you can afford in terms of lifestyle.

To do this, here's a simple outline you can follow:

First, write down your total income. Let's pick an easy, round number, say, $50,000.

Next, subtract how much you feel you are supposed to give. Let's assume we're going to give a full tithe, or 10 percent, of our gross income. So 10 percent of $50,000 is $5,000. This leaves a balance of $45,000.

Then subtract taxes. On a salary of $50,000, that could be anywhere from 18 to 25 percent, so let's say taxes will be about $10,000. We now have $35,000 left to work with.

Next, subtract your annual debt repayment. This amount changes from person to person, so let's just pick a number, say, $5,000.

Next, subtract the amount you want to invest in long-term savings. Most financial advisors would suggest about 10 percent.

So that would be another $5,000.

Now after you've subtracted your giving, taxes, debt repayment, and savings, you have a figure that reflects how much you have to fund your lifestyle. It's $25,000.

And that's the figure we would have to live off of for our *lifestyle*.[6]

But here's our natural tendency—myself included. *We don't do this.* In fact, we do just the opposite. We start off by listing how we want to live in terms of lifestyle: the house we want, the clothes we want to wear, how often we want to eat out, the number of TV sets in place. Then we subtract the debt repayments needed to *fund* that lifestyle. Then we take out taxes, and then we try to save something (which is usually little or nothing). And giving? It can get overlooked almost entirely. Instead of giving God a tithe, we end up giving Him a tip—five dollars here, ten dollars there, a few hundred now and then, and then try not to think about it too much. But a God-honoring spending plan doesn't begin with lifestyle; it begins with *commitments* and *priorities*. It reflects the reality that God owns it all, and we are the managers. It is directed by the reality that any financial decision is a spiritual decision and that one day we will be held accountable for our management. A good spending plan has a single motivation: to experience a truly spiritual life.

GETTING STARTED

So what do you do if you want to take this route, but your figures don't add up? What do you do if your expenses exceed your income? Let's go back to where our money goes. Can you cut taxes? Maybe a little here and there with some creative homework, but by and large you are in a particular bracket and you have to pay a fairly consistent amount. The main way you cut taxes is to reduce your income, which isn't exactly high on anybody's list.

Are you going to cut giving? Well, that depends on your priorities. I once heard of a farmer who promised to give God one of the twin calves his cow delivered. His wife asked him, "Which calf is the Lord's?"

"It really doesn't make any difference whose calf is whose," the farmer answered. "I'm just going to give God one of them when they're grown."

A few weeks later the farmer came into the farmhouse with a long, sad face.

"What's wrong?" his wife asked anxiously.

"Well," he said, "the Lord's calf died this morning."

Tempting, isn't it? And it's often how we think and act, but it reveals a life without principle, commitment, or trust. So can you cut out your debt repayment? Actually, paying off your debt is the best thing you have *going* for you.

So what's left? *Lifestyle!* Now many lifestyle issues can't be changed, such as the number of children you have. But many lifestyle issues *can* be changed *if we're willing to change them.* And the heart of the change is simple: *Spend less.* If the lifestyle issue isn't addressed, then with every increase in income, you'll simply increase your level of lifestyle without gaining a single inch of ground toward honoring God with your money and freeing yourself up for spiritual growth and health.

A good spending plan doesn't begin with lifestyle, but with commitments, priorities, and the principles that God gives. That's why Jesus said, "No one can serve two masters. Either he will hate the one and love the other, or he will be devoted to the one and despise the other. You cannot serve both God and Money" (Matt. 6:24). For most of us, getting on track will take spending less than we earn and doing it for a long time. The key is to begin a gradual implementation of God's plan, even with small steps. When you've been operating on a different set of principles, it's easy to think, *I can't do this! I can't even live off of 100 percent of the money I'm making now, much less what I'd be bringing home if I set aside money for a tithe or savings!* Or you may have already gone overboard with debt and can't see a way out. The mistake would be to bag the whole thing because you aren't able to implement it *fully* from the beginning. Don't do that. What most financial planners would suggest, and what I am convinced is thoroughly God-honoring, is to move toward this *gradually.* For example, take the tithe: Start with 2, 3, or 5 percent, with a commitment to increase this amount later to a full 10 percent or more as you improve your financial standing and balance out your spending plan from older priorities and previous spending decisions. The point is to *begin the process,* because it matters. Where you place your treasure is where you place your heart.

ARE YOU LIKE GOD?

Shortly after World War II came to a close, Europe began to pick up the pieces. Much of its land had been ravaged by war and was in ruins. Perhaps the most tragic aftershock of all was the large number of orphaned children left starving in the streets. One morning, an American soldier was making his way back to his barracks in London. As he turned a corner in his jeep, he saw a little boy pressing his nose against the window of a bakery. Inside, the cook was making bread for doughnuts. The hungry boy stared in silence, watching every move. The soldier stopped his jeep, got out, and walked over to where the little boy was standing. Together they watched the doughnuts come out of the oven and then placed— steaming—inside a glass counter. The soldier's heart went out to the little boy, so he said, "Son, would you like some of those?"

"Oh, yes, I would!" the boy said.

So the soldier stepped inside and bought a dozen of the hot, fresh morsels, put them in a bag, and walked back out and handed them to the boy. As he turned to get back in his jeep, he felt a little tug on his coat. It was the little boy.

"What is it, son?"

"Mister," the boy said, "are you God?"[7]

It's understandable why he'd think that way, isn't it? Nothing reflects who we are more tangibly than how we manage our money. And when we manage our money as God would have it, particularly in the area of giving, we become like Him.

1. Why does a person's relationship with money reveal that person's heart and character?

2. What is God's foundational financial principle? (See page 154.) What difference should that principle make in how a Christian deals with money?

3. What does God get from tithing? What does the giver receive?

4. What examples can you give of times in your life when you have seen God outgiving you?

CHAPTER TEN

Impacting a Destiny

Why are you reading a book on spiritual living? I know why I am *writing* one on the spiritual life. It began with a mother who encouraged me to be a spiritual seeker. She introduced me to Christianity, as well as to her own spiritual pilgrimage. And then, largely because I was kicked out of the public school for being a bit disruptive, I was put in a private Christian school in the second grade. And in that school was a second-grade teacher—the principal's wife, no less—by the name of Mrs. Shedd. She worked hard on me and gave me my first Bible. And then, many years later, a group of Christian friends in college built a relationship with me—Mike, Mel, and Terry. They cared about me, reached out to me, and invited me to an InterVarsity Christian Fellowship meeting, and eventually I went. And at that meeting, I turned my life over to the leadership of Christ. That's why I'm writing this book. I can walk you through the names and faces that led me to this point, and I will be forever grateful. Now, back to you: Why are you reading this book? Who are the people who shaped your spiritual pilgrimage? Whoever they were, they were engaged in an enterprise that did nearly as much for them as it did for you—and that enterprise is evangelism. Just clocked out on me, didn't you?

I once heard a speaker play a little word-association game along these lines.[1] I'm going to give you a word, and you see what image comes into your mind. Ready?

Librarian.

Got a picture in your mind? Mine was of a little old lady with her hair in a bun.

Here's another one: *Sumo wrestler.*

What came to mind? Five-hundred-pound guy in diapers, right?

Fighter pilot.

Women instantly picture Tom Cruise from the movie *Top Gun.* All us guys think of ourselves.

Now what picture comes to your mind when I say the word *evangelist?* Probably some animated, Bible-thumping, fire-'n'-brimstone, obnoxious, pushy, self-righteous type who leans toward polyester as a fashion statement. So when I bring up evangelism as a component to experiencing a spiritual life, your temptation is to move on to the next section. Talking about your faith with others can be uncomfortable and awkward. You don't want to offend anyone or come across as being a religious fanatic. It's also common to feel that since faith is such a private matter, it shouldn't be brought up or suggested to another person. Sometimes we just feel that it's not our role, that evangelism is the responsibility of a professional minister.

The High-Yield Investment of Evangelism

Yet you are where you are at spiritually today because somebody, somewhere, did feel like it was his business. He wasn't embarrassed or awkward, had the courage to risk your ridicule or rejection, took the time and effort to find out how to talk about his faith, went out of his comfort zone, built a relationship with you, and never *once* felt like it was someone else's job. And that person reaped an enormous spiritual reward as a result. Why?

Evangelism Deepens Your Spiritual Life

When you talk about your faith with someone, it deepens your own understanding of your faith. You can't help but go a little bit deeper as to *why* you believe *what* you believe. When you make your faith known to others, they're going to ask you all kinds of questions that you may have never thought of—good questions, honest questions, ones worth answering. And investing what it will take to give them answers will put your faith through a workout that will build its strength.

Evangelism Brings Accountability to Your Spiritual Life

A second benefit of evangelism is that it will bring accountability to your spiritual life. It's easy to become comfortable believing one way but then living another or having what you believe become a side issue, marginalized, or even trivialized, compared to other concerns. But when you're in a relationship with someone who is considering a faith decision and dialoguing with you about *yours,* it brings an accountability and challenge to your life that wouldn't have come in any other way. Your spirituality comes under examination in the best and healthiest of ways.

Evangelism Energizes Your Spiritual Life

Third, evangelism energizes your spiritual life. Your prayers take on a new edge; your reading of the Bible has added meaning; the weekend service that you invited your friend to attend gains a level of significance and importance that was missing before. Evangelism is like a shot of adrenaline through your spiritual system.

But that's just how you're energized through the *process*—there's also the potential of this investment taking you to a new high by delivering one of the greatest spiritual moments you can ever experience: becoming an instrument in a changed life. There is nothing like having someone say, "I was lost, and now I'm found; I was blind, but now I can see; I was squandering my life, and now it has purpose and meaning; I was searching, and now I'm home." And then they look at you, and say, "And God used *you* to do it." Christians believe that there really is an eternal destiny for every human being. We believe that our choices in this life have consequences, that heaven and hell are real, and that real people—people with names, faces, and families—will go to one place or the other. And when one of those people makes a decision to enter into spiritual life through Christ, it's like rescuing someone from a burning car. It really is saving a life. And it just doesn't get any better than that.

A young woman on the staff of our church named Kristina is dear to me. We kid each other that she is my third daughter. And in many ways, she is my daughter, because I was used by God to bring her to Christ and the Christian faith. In fact, she was the first person who became a Christian through the ministry of our church. Kristina attended our very first service when we were meeting in a Hilton hotel. On the fourth week, I presented the essence of the message of the Christian faith—that people like her mattered to God, that Jesus had died for her sins and wanted to forgive her and be in relationship with her. When I asked, "Is there anyone here who would like to accept that gift, to begin that relationship?" Kristina said, "Yes. I would."

And then, just a few weeks later, I baptized her. Our practice is for folks to write out a paragraph or two of their journey toward faith in Christ and then to have that read as part of their baptism. Kristina didn't do that. Instead, she wanted to sing a song. And she sang a song called "Thank You," with lyrics that said, "Thank you for giving to the Lord. I am a life that was changed. . . . I am so glad you gave."[2]

I've watched that precious young woman grow up in her faith, find and develop her spiritual gifts, and put them into our programming ministry, which utilizes the arts for weekend and midweek services. I've seen her meet and fall in love with a godly man, resulting in my officiating at their wedding. Then came their first child, and I almost burst into tears when I dedicated that child to God: All I could think of was our life journey together—and what *could* have been! What if Kristina hadn't been invited to that first service? What if I had never talked to her about spiritual things? *What if?* Both of our lives would have lost more than words could ever convey—me, a dear daughter; Kristina, a life with God and an eternity in heaven.

If you have experienced the joy and the thrill of being a part of a changed life, would you trade a single moment? Was there anything like it when you saw that friend, that family member, that person from work emerge from the waters of baptism and then come up to you and say, "Thanks. Thanks for taking the risk, thanks for answering my questions, thanks for not being ashamed of your faith in Christ. I am a life that's been changed"? And if you *haven't* experienced this yet, can you see what you're missing?

How We Can Impact a Destiny

Now here's the good news—you can engage in evangelism, reaping all of its rewards, without being like the image that came to your mind during our word-association game. I think this undesirable image is what trips us up so much. We don't want to barge into someone's life uninvited or seem pushy or obnoxious. We hate it when people are like that to us, and we don't want to be that way to others. But being an evangelist is not what you think.

I once heard of a little four-year-old boy who was asked to be the ring bearer at a wedding. The day came, and he was all dressed up in his little tuxedo. When his time came to walk the aisle, every head turned to watch. Then, with all eyes on him, he scrunched up his face and said, "Grrrr! Grrrr!" with his hands held up in front of his face, making a clawing movement all the way down the aisle! He then went through the entire wedding ceremony with perfect behavior—no noises, no growls, no faces, and no gestures. He was a perfect little gentleman. Then came the recessional, and as he walked back down the aisle, the ferocious animal impersonation returned. "Grrrr! Grrrr!"—all the way down! When the wedding was over, they found out why—he thought that he was asked to be the ring "bear," not "bearer."[3]

It's easy to get the wrong idea about what we're being asked to do, isn't it? When I first heard about evangelism, my initial thought was that I would have to knock on people's doors, hand out tracts on a street corner, or be obnoxious and pushy with people at work. And it didn't help that one of the first experiences I ever had with someone who was trying to be an ambassador for Christ was a little less than helpful.

I was a sophomore in college and had just given my life to Christ. I was invited to a weekend retreat with some other folks from a campus ministry, so I went. The retreat ended on a Sunday, and before we left, we decided we would go to church together. I was all dressed up, Bible in hand, but I had a few moments before it was time to leave—so I walked over to a drink machine. I put in my money, pushed the button, and when I bent down to get the can, I heard—and felt—this *rip* in my pants!

I'm not talking about your average, everyday, little rip. I'm talking about the kind of rip you can hear two blocks away and large enough to let everyone know *exactly* what brand of underwear you wear. So there I was, bent over, not believing this was happening, when out of nowhere comes this woman—from behind, of course—named Karen, who was one of the staff workers for the retreat.

"I see you've got kind of a problem," she said.

"You see very well," I replied.

"You want me to take you someplace and get that sewed up?"

"You know," I said, "that would probably rank pretty high with me right now."

So we jumped in her car and started down the road. At first I didn't say anything—conversation, you would understand, wasn't exactly on my mind. I assumed she lived nearby and we were going to her house for a quick repair job. Then I noticed that she was looking up and down every street, searching, glancing, as if she didn't know where she was going.

Then it struck me: I was in a car with my underwear hanging out with a stranger who told me she was taking me somewhere— and she didn't seem to know where!

So finally I asked her, "Do you know where we are going?"

"No," she replied pleasantly.

And all I could muster in my shock was, "Oh." And she didn't say anything else, and neither did I, for several miles. But then, being a master of communication, I said, "So where . . . uh . . . exactly, are we going?"

Then she said—and I am *not* making this up—"I'm looking for someone walking out for the Sunday morning paper so that we can pull in and ask to use that person's sewing machine. Don't you think that would be a great way to get to know someone who may not know the Lord?"

And all I could think was, *No, I don't!*

But before I could tell her that wasn't my style of evangelism, especially with my underwear not being my favorite opening line, she spotted some old lady coming out of her house and whipped her Volkswagen in the driveway. And in a state of shock I heard her say, "Excuse me, we were on our way to church, and he split his pants. Do you have a sewing machine we could use?"

And what killed me was this lady said, "Sure, come on in!"

Before I knew it, I was standing in my underwear in some strange lady's bathroom—with her poodle, no less—listening to Karen try to tell this woman about Jesus while she sewed up my pants. Forgive me, but I walked away thinking, *If that's what it means to do evangelism, count me out.* Fortunately for us all, it wasn't.

When it comes to evangelism, here's what you're *really* being asked to do—it's just three simple steps, all of which you can see in the life of a man in the Bible named Andrew: "Andrew, Simon Peter's brother, was one of the two who heard what John had said and who had followed Jesus. The first thing Andrew did was to find his brother Simon and tell him, 'We have found the Messiah' (that is, the Christ). And he brought him to Jesus" (John 1:40–42).

Build a Relationship

The first step that Andrew took was relational. The Bible says that when Andrew made the decision to follow Jesus, and he found in that relationship spiritual truth and meaning, he immediately went to someone he was in a relationship with and reached out to him in the context of that relationship. This step is no more, but no less, than reaching out to our friends, family members, neighbors, or coworkers. It's connecting with people we see at the gym, the playground, or the Little-League field. It's relating to the person who cuts our hair, does our dry cleaning, or baby-sits our kids.

Be Willing to Share

The second step that Andrew took, within the context of his relationship with Peter, was to communicate something about what he had discovered for his own life. He shared about his spiritual life and talked about his spiritual decisions. In this instance, it was with his brother, and he just said, "Listen, Pete, this guy Jesus is the One we've been searching for!" To take the second step and actually communicate something doesn't mean you say something forced or artificial or give some kind of prepared speech. It just means you have an openness about your faith in the context of your relationships, and, when the opportunity presents itself, you share who and what you're about, including your spiritual life and what that spiritual life is all about.

The Bible tells of an Ethiopian man who wanted to explore Christianity. One day he turned to a Christian and asked, "How can I [understand] . . . unless someone explains it to me?" (Acts 8:31). And he was right—how could he? Now when the door opens like this, it can lead to a full-blown dialogue—one that allows you to enter into an authentic, compelling conversation about what Christ means to you, what He's done in your life, and what He can do in that person's life. But most of the time, your sharing will initially be casual remarks here and there, small statements that find their way into the conversation, letting that person get to know you and the orientation of your life. These will be windows into your soul that will let them see Christ residing in the home of your heart.

Recently I was in a conversation with a guy I was just beginning to get to know. We met because our sons were on the same basketball team at the YMCA. We never got to talk for long, but we liked each other. I had no idea where this guy was at spiritually, but I began to pray that I could somehow find out and perhaps begin talking with him about spiritual things. Then, just a few weeks into our relationship, he asked me what I did for a living. As a minister, that question has a tendency to move the conversation in a particular direction.

"I pastor a church here in Charlotte," I said.

And he said, "Really!" like he couldn't believe it, because up to that point he had thought of me as a relatively normal person. (Ministers are often classified as something akin to a third sex.) Then he started talking about his church background, his mother's involvement in church, and a bit about where he was currently. So there we were, talking about spiritual things in the context of a new friendship, *and it was the most natural thing in the world.*

All it took was my willingness to openly go wherever the conversation took things, including who I was in Christ. So how might this play out with you? Maybe something like this: A friend says, "Hey, how was your weekend? Did you have a good one?" A simple, natural, but potentially life-changing answer could be, "Well, we went out Friday night, saw a movie. Saturday, I cut the lawn and grilled out and played some with the kids. Sunday, we went to church—had a great time there. Really interesting talk. Made me think, and gave me some stuff I can really use. So yeah, good weekend." Nothing forced, just the reality of who you are. And, as the relationship develops over time, that kind of authenticity will open up all kinds of dialogue about spiritual things in a natural, open, and positive way.[4] And no matter how limited you think your ability to share you faith may be, don't ever underestimate its impact on those around you.

There was a little boy named Billy who had cerebral palsy, so his brain was unable to exercise proper control over the movements of his body and his speech. He attended a middle-school summer camp, and the other kids took great delight in making fun of him. They called him "spastic." It often seems that we human beings have our most cruel period of life in junior high. As Billy would walk around the camp, the other campers would line up behind him, imitating his handicapped walk, mimicking his every movement.

They thought it was funny.

Once, when asking another boy for directions to the craft shop, the other boy twisted up his face grotesquely in a cruel impersonation of Billy's face, pointed a dozen different ways, and said, "That way!" in the slurred speech Billy's body could not help but produce.

One Wednesday morning, Billy's cabin had been assigned camp devotions. They had to choose someone to stand in front of 150 kids and speak. The boys in Billy's cabin voted unanimously for him. They knew he couldn't do it, but in their cruel sense of humor, they thought it would be fun to see "spastic Billy" give it a try. Surprisingly, little Billy agreed.

That evening, as he limped his way to the podium, the boys began their mocking laughter and sneering. When Billy got to the front, he began to speak. It took him almost ten tortured minutes to say just one sentence:

"Je-sus loves meee . . . Je-Je-Je-sus loves meee . . . annd-I-I-love Je-Je-Jesus!"

When he finished, there was dead silence. Boys who minutes before had been jeering and laughing were now shaking and trembling. Something happened that night: God swept over that room, and boy after boy turned his life over to Christ's leadership— all because a spastic boy named Billy decided to do what didn't come very naturally or easily: He told others about his faith. And it mattered.[5]

Extend an Invitation

Then comes the third step. Look back at our encounter with Andrew—he didn't just build the relationship and then communicate something casually to his brother about Jesus or his decision to follow Jesus. He did a third thing: *He brought Peter to Jesus.* He invited him to come and see and hear. People do not often come to church and explore Christianity through a pamphlet left in a bathroom, a billboard sign, a radio or TV show, or even an ad in the paper. They come because someone *invited* them. And today, more and more churches are investing in making that invitation a potent one, designing services to present the basic truths of the Christian faith to those who come from an unchurched background but are open to spiritual exploration. And guess what: Studies show that 50 percent of all Americans—people who are our friends, family members, neighbors, and coworkers—would come to church if only they were invited by someone they knew.

Fifty percent.

ONE MAN'S IMPACT

Ken Gire writes of a man by the name of Scott Manley who reached out to high-school students on the campus of Arlington Heights High School in the late sixties. "He showed up in a pair of Converse All-Stars, gym shorts, T-shirt, a handshake, and a smile. Several of us on the basketball team were playing a pickup game in the gym, and this young seminary student from Southwestern Baptist Theological Seminary worked his way into the game. Over the weeks ahead he kept showing up. At lunch. After school. In the parking lot. And before long, he worked his way into our lives."

Scott was working through a ministry called Young Life, which builds relationships with high-school students, establishes clubs, and sponsors Bible study groups, all for the purpose of reaching out with the saving message of Christ in places where churches often cannot go. Ken reflects that he doesn't remember any of Scott's talks, only the music of the message: *I love you. I care about you. You matter. Your pain matters. Your struggles matter. Your life is sacred and dear to God. He has a future for you, plans and hopes and dreams and blessings for you.* And the music streamed into Ken's heart. Ken became a Christian, going on to Texas Christian University, where he, in turn, led a Young Life club. Also on the leadership team was a young woman named Judy, who would one day become Ken's wife. Judy had become a Christian through a classmate, who had become a Christian through her Young Life leader, who had become a Christian through . . . *Scott Manley.*

One day Ken and Judy ran into Scott at a conference they were attending together, along with three of their four children. Judy, who had never met Scott, approached him and said, "You don't know me, but I'm Judy Gire, Ken Gire's wife." They hugged, then she continued. "There's something I've been wanting to tell you for a long time." Years of emotion welled inside her. "Scott, you were instrumental in leading my husband to Christ. You led my Young Life leader to Christ. My Young Life leader led a friend of mine to Christ. And this friend told me about Christ. You are my spiritual heritage. These are three of my children. This is Kelly, and she knows Jesus. This is Rachel, and she knows Jesus. This is Stephen, and he knows Jesus. And Gretchen, our oldest, she isn't here, but she knows Jesus too. All of us know Jesus because of Scott Manley. Thank you so much. Thank you."

Scott threw his arms around her, and for a long time they wept together.[6]

Don't let evangelism scare you or put you off. It's one of the most important and rewarding investments a person can ever make—not only for your own spirituality, but for the spiritual lives of others in our world. Just ask Ken and Judy. Or ask me. Even better, just ask yourself.

Samuel Shoemaker, who was instrumental in the development of Alcoholics Anonymous, once wrote a poem that captures the importance of this for us all:

> *I stay near the door.*
> *I neither go too far in, nor stay too far out.*
> *The door is the most important door in the world—*
> *It is the door through which people walk when they*
>   *find God.*
> *There's no use my going way inside, and staying there,*
> *When so many are still outside and they, as much as I,*
> *Crave to know where the door is.*
> *And all that so many ever find*
> *Is only the wall where a door ought to be.*
> *They creep along the wall like blind people,*
> *With outstretched, groping hands,*
> *Feeling for a door, knowing there must be a door,*
> *Yet they never find it . . .*
> *So I stay near the door.*
> *The most tremendous thing in the world*
> *Is for people to find that door—the door to God.*
> *The most important thing anyone can do*
> *Is to take hold of one of those blind, groping hands,*
> *And to put it on the latch—the latch that only clicks*
> *And opens to the person's own touch.*

People die outside that door, as starving beggars die
On cold nights in cruel cities in the dead of winter—
Die for want of what is within their grasp.
They live, on the other side of it—live because they have
found it.
Nothing else matters compared to helping them find it,
And open it, and walk in, and find Him . . .
So I stay near the door.[7]

---

1. Who first shared with you about Christ? Who has recently been a great spiritual encouragement to you?

2. Who do you think you might be able to encourage spiritually?

3. If someone were to watch you for a week, how would they know that you are a Christian?

4. What character quality in a Christian would most attract someone else to consider Christ?

CHAPTER ELEVEN

The Committed Life

My sister sent me something off the Internet a few years ago that she thought I would find funny. It was an excerpt from a home-economics textbook used in the fifties. This passage is from the chapter on how a woman should act when her husband comes home from work:

> Have dinner ready. Plan ahead, even the night before, to have a delicious meal—on time. This is a way of letting him know that you have been thinking about him and are concerned about his needs. Most men are hungry when they come home and the prospects of a good meal are part of the warm welcome needed.
>
> Prepare yourself. Take 15 minutes to rest so you will be refreshed when he arrives. Touch up your makeup, put a ribbon in your hair and be fresh looking. . . . Be a little gay and a little more interesting.

[Hold on, it gets worse.]

Clear away the clutter . . . run a dust cloth over the tables. Your husband will feel he has reached a haven of rest and order. Prepare the children. Take a few minutes to wash the children's hand and faces, comb their hair, and if necessary, change their clothes. They are little treasures and he would like to see them playing the part.

[Here's my favorite part.]

Make him comfortable. Have him lean back in a comfortable chair or suggest he lie down in the bedroom. Have a cool or warm drink ready for him. Arrange his pillow and offer to take off his shoes. Speak in a low, soft, soothing and pleasant voice. Make the evening his: never complain if he does not take you out to dinner or to other places of entertainment . . . the goal: a place where your husband can renew himself.[1]

Actually, now that I reread that, it doesn't sound so bad! Fortunately for my wife, I didn't get what I learned about marriage from a book like that. When I was in college, I attended a filmed series of lectures by a Christian psychologist who talked about how to build a strong and lasting marriage. It was healthy, balanced, practical, and based on solid principles that were taken straight from the Bible. But at the end of the series, I realized something. All that I had been learning about marriage depended on one little thing—whether I was ever going to get *married!* It was great to learn how to strengthen marital communication, how to work through marital conflict, how to nurture marital intimacy—but ultimately, I had to decide whether I was ever going to be marital! And that's why this final chapter is so crucial, because it raises an all-determining question: Are you going to be *committed?* Because until that has been settled, all of the things we've talked about throughout this book—things like quiet times, strategic spiritual relationships, serving, money, and worship—become empty head knowledge or, at best, something you'll dabble in here and there but never let direct the course of your life.

Commitment is everything.

It's no wonder, then, that when you look at the life of Jesus, He was relentless about this subject. He would never let conversation on how people could develop themselves spiritually get very far before raising the greater issue: whether they were willing to be spiritual. Because their commitment, more than anything, determined whether they would ever experience a truly spiritual life.

Tony Campolo, who for years was a professor at the University of Pennsylvania and now teaches at Eastern College, says that every year, usually in May, students come into his office, look at him across the desk, and say, "Doc, I'm not coming back next semester."

Campolo then whips off his glasses, tries to look "professorial," and says, "Dear student, tell me why?"

They always look at him with a strained look and say, "I need *time*, Doc, I need *time.*"

Campolo says he thinks to himself, *This guy's done nothing with his life for the last six months—and now he needs time?* But the student goes on, saying, "I need time to find myself. I'm tired of playing all these roles that society says I have to play. I'm tired of being who my friends expect me to be, who my parents expect me to be, who the system expects me to be. I've got to peel away each of these socially prescribed roles. I've got to peel them away—do you hear?—and come to grips with the core of my being, the essence of my personality!"

Tony says he now responds to this with a simple question to the student: "Friend, suppose after you peel away each of these socially prescribed identities, after you peel away each of these socially created selves, you discover you are an onion!" You peel away all of the skins of the onion, and what's left? Nothing! The onion is nothing more than the sum total of its skins. "So could it be," Campolo continues, "that you are nothing more than the sum total of all of the roles society has trained you to play. And after you peel away each of those selves and take the long journey into who you really are—your inner self—you'll get there and discover that 'Hi-ho, nobody's home!'"[2]

I think Campolo's on to something. There's a common idea floating around in our world that everybody has a true, inner "self" just waiting to be discovered. I don't think that's true. Who we are is not something waiting to be found; who we are is something waiting to be *created*. And we are created *by* commitment and *for* commitment.

In his newspaper column called "Market Report," Bill Barnhart once talked about the difference between investors and traders in the stock market. He says that a trader makes decisions on a minute-by-minute basis, wheeling and dealing, pursuing short-term profits.

Traders may have no confidence whatsoever in the companies in which they buy stock. All they're after is an immediate payoff. An investor, on the other hand, buys stock based on his views of the company. Investors are in it for the long haul. They chain themselves to the mast. They commit their money to a stock, believing that over time, the stock will pay dividends and grow in value. The ups and downs of the market don't scare them, because they believe in the quality of the company, its leaders, and its product.[3]

When it comes to your spiritual life in Christ, you have to decide whether you are going to be an investor or a trader. Which you choose will determine *everything*. Following Jesus is not an idea, much less a philosophy. It's a tangible, life-changing *act*. It's something that you *do*. It's a fundamental, settled choice within your very being—a choice that not everyone who desires a spiritual life is willing to make.

THREE ENCOUNTERS

The following is a provocative series of encounters, captured by Luke, between Jesus and those who desired the benefits of a spiritual life:

> As they were walking along the road, a man said to [Jesus], "I will follow you wherever you go."
>
> Jesus replied, "Foxes have holes and birds of the air have nests, but the Son of Man has no place to lay his head."
>
> He said to another man, "Follow me."

But the man replied, "Lord, first let me go and bury my father."

Jesus said to him, "Let the dead bury their own dead, but you go and proclaim the kingdom of God."

Still another said, "I will follow you, Lord; but first let me go back and say good-by to my family."

Jesus replied, "No one who puts his hand to the plow and looks back is fit for service in the kingdom of God." (Luke 9:57–62)

Here were three people who each wrestled with the issue of following Jesus. The first seemed to be willing. He was quick to say, "Count me in! Wherever, whenever, however." And you'd think that Jesus would be thrilled that someone would have that kind of attitude. But did you notice how Jesus responded? In essence, He said, "I don't think you get it." To choose to follow Jesus means to know what it is you're choosing and *then* to make the choice. Jesus knew that commitment was not to be taken lightly; once He even said, "If anyone would come after me, he must deny himself and take up his cross daily and follow me" (Luke 9:23). For Jesus, that language wasn't just demonstrating a flair for the dramatic. For Him, it was literal. He knew that His cross was real—an instrument of ancient, cruel torture that resulted in humiliation; raw, excruciating pain; blood; ripped flesh; and eventual death. Christian spirituality isn't about sitting at the feet of some guru for a seminar at a retreat. It isn't about having a nice, comfortable, safe dose of spirituality in your life to make you feel good whenever your thoughts run deep about ultimate questions and eternal destinies. Jesus called people to *follow* Him—and there was only one place where He was going: *a cross*. The true nature of spiritual living involves sacrifice, duty, and commitment.

Then there's the second person Jesus encountered. This person wanted a spiritual life, but he wanted to put off what it would take, or at least put the investment on hold. When the second man said that he wanted to go back to bury his father, he didn't mean he simply wanted to go back and attend to his dad's funeral. He used a Hebrew phrase that meant that he wanted to go back and *wait* for his father to die. He wanted to be available in case there was anything he needed to do whenever his father *did* die. His father may not have even been ill! He was saying that his life, with its issues and concerns and responsibilities, was more important than following Jesus. So when it came to the call to follow Christ, he said, "Not now, Jesus; it's kind of a bad time for me. My life's really full, and I've got a lot on my plate. But I really want to *give* to You; I really do want to put You first. But right now is just not a good time."

And look at how Jesus replied: "Let the dead bury the dead." To paraphrase Jesus, "Let those who are spiritually lifeless order their life around things that don't have any eternal significance. You show signs of life—or at least act like you *want* to be alive—so *live* like it! Let those who care more about the material world than the spiritual world build their lives and commitments and decisions around goals and efforts and investments that won't matter at the end of a life. I'm calling you to invest in the kingdom of God. And that's not an investment for a season, but the investment of a life." Jesus' reply, in short, was "put up or shut up."

And then there was the third guy. He didn't jump in and say yes without thinking about the cost. He didn't put Jesus off and say, "Well, maybe later." The third guy had a different twist—he said, "Okay, I'll follow you, *but* . . ." And then he inserted a qualification about the *degree* to which he would follow. Now in his case, the qualification seemed reasonable, didn't it? All he wanted to do was go and say good-bye to his family. But that wasn't what was really going on. The issue wasn't saying good-bye. We can see that from how Jesus responded to him. Jesus saw right through this guy's words to what was really going on—it wasn't about saying good-bye to his family; it was about not wanting to say good-bye to his previous way of life. He wanted to say yes to Jesus while holding on to what he *had* been following and to the priorities he *used* to pursue. And Jesus' reply made it very clear that He had no use for that kind of following.

To follow Jesus means that your heart is *fully His,* not divided in its loyalties. Jesus didn't want little professions and halfhearted commitments or weak, watered-down, limp-wristed responses. He didn't want people to think that following Him was something tame that people could do in their spare time. Following Him could never be a matter of "Yes, *but*—let me do this, or not do that, go back here, cling to this, keep doing that." Jesus said, in essence, "You want just enough spirituality to feel good about yourself, but not enough to change your life. That's not what following Me is about."

Interesting, isn't it? Not a single one of these men wanted to turn Jesus down. Not a single one said, "Heck no, I don't want to follow You." They *wanted* what they knew in their hearts following would bring to their lives. They wanted to feel good about themselves spiritually and to develop themselves spiritually. They wanted Jesus in their lives. What they *didn't* want to do was what it would take—*commitment.* This is one of the great ironies in life. As Tom Landry once said, as head football coach of the Dallas Cowboys, his job was to get a group of men to do what they didn't want to do so they could achieve the one thing they had wanted all their lives.

THE STRUGGLE TO COMMIT

This is why in the Bible we find a place where God, through the prophet Jeremiah, asked an extremely important question of people who had become spiritually alive, but not much else: "Who is he who will devote himself to be close to me?" (Jer. 30:21).

So why is commitment so hard? Why don't we do what it takes to have what we say we most want? I think there are three reasons. The first reason is because we don't truly *care* about what the commitment would bring. We'd like the spiritual life we see in others to be in our own but not enough to do what it takes to have it. It's as if we've decided to settle for about twenty dollars' worth of God, just enough to make us feel good about ourselves. We see others who have bought into God a little more, and every now and then it crosses our mind to increase our investment, but then the feeling

197

passes and we settle for our twenty dollars' worth.[4] Why? We don't value our spiritual life as much as we say we do.

In the late fifties and early sixties, when Khrushchev was head of the Communist Party in Russia, there was a severe crisis in corn production. So Khrushchev gathered all of the corn producers of the country into one huge auditorium in order to address the problem head-on. Standing before the large number of people, Khrushchev began by thundering one solitary question: "How many of you here today believe we need to be committed to solving the corn-production problem in our country?"

A huge forest of hands shot up!

Khrushchev, who was a good public speaker, simply stared at them. He said nothing. Moment after uncomfortable moment passed by without their leader saying a word.

Suddenly he said, "Then where is the corn?"[5]

He knew that if they really *had* been committed, they would have something to show for it.

A second reason we struggle with commitment is because we don't want what commitment brings—namely, *obedience*. We have beliefs, behaviors, practices, and priorities within our lives that we know wouldn't mix with true commitment—and we've chosen to cling to them over God. Jesus had a swift challenge to this position: "So why do you call me 'Lord,' when you won't obey me?" (Luke 6:46 NLT). Jesus is saying that if you're not going to obey Him, stop saying that He's your Lord, because it's obvious that He's not.

A third reason we shy away from commitment is because we're *afraid*. We'd like to give our lives over to God, but when we see the risk that comes with it and the trust we'd have to have, we give in to fear and decide not to take the plunge. But that's where faith comes in—not blind faith nor a faith built on wishful thinking, but faith built on God Himself. I once read an interview of a circus trapeze artist. The conversation turned to the daring stunts that he performed and the importance of having a net underneath. The trapeze artist admitted that the net was there to keep them from breaking their necks, but then he added that it also *kept* him from falling. When the reporter asked him why, he said, "Imagine that there is no net. We would be so nervous that we would be more likely to miss and fall. If there wasn't a net, we would not dare to do some of the things we do. But because there is a net, we can make two turns—sometimes three!"[6]

God is our net. And because of Him, we can always take the risk of commitment.

I ran across an old book once that has now become a prized part of my library. It was a biography, simply titled *Borden of Yale*. It told of a man named William Borden, who went to Yale University as an undergraduate and later became a missionary candidate for China. When he made his decision to invest his life in Christian ministry, many of his friends thought he had made a mistake. He had come from a good family. He had money and one of the finest educations in the land. And because of his background, countless people came to him and asked, "Why are you going to throw your life away in some foreign country when you can have such an enjoyable and worthwhile life here?" But Borden had heard a call from God, and he decided not to just hear it, but to obey it.

While in Egypt, before he ever got to China, Borden became deathly ill. Soon it was evident to everyone, including himself, that he would die. At that point, Borden could have said, "What a waste! My friends were right! I could have stayed home!"

But Borden didn't think that way. As he laid on his deathbed in Egypt, he scribbled a farewell note to his friends that had the following six words: "No reserve, no retreat, and no regrets."[7]

A LONG JOURNEY IN THE SAME DIRECTION

A spiritual life is a long journey in the same direction.[8] It begins with a single step, but it only progresses as additional steps are taken. And those that go the furthest are those who are the most committed.

One of the top stories for the end of the nineties was Michael Jordan's retirement from professional basketball. I once heard someone talk about going to the United Center in Chicago to watch Jordan and the Bulls play a basketball game. He got there pretty early, and when he arrived, he saw something interesting. Forty-five minutes before the practice and shoot-around, Michael Jordan—arguably the greatest basketball player that has ever played the game—was *practicing*. All alone on the court, Jordan was working on something that he thought *needed* work. Nobody made him do that. Just Jordan. And that's why he's made such an impact. Because if you know anything about Jordan's career, you know that he didn't start off as a successful player. In fact, he was cut from his high-school basketball team. What made the difference in Jordan's life? *Commitment.*

Or think of Gary Player, who won more international golf tournaments in his day than anyone else. When Player was competing in a tournament, people constantly came up to him and made the same remark: "I'd give anything if I could hit a golf ball like you."

On one particularly tough day, Player was tired and frustrated when, once again, he heard the comment: "I'd give anything if I could hit a golf ball like you." Player's usual politeness failed him as he replied to the spectator, "No, you wouldn't. You'd give anything to hit a golf ball like me if it were easy. Do you know what you've got to do to hit a golf ball like me? You've got to get up at five o'clock in the morning, go out on the course, and hit a thousand golf balls. Your hand starts bleeding, and you walk up to the clubhouse, wash the blood off your hand, slap a bandage on it, and go out and hit another thousand golf balls. That's what it takes to hit a golf ball like me."

Only within the context of a committed relationship does Jesus promise to reveal Himself to us and show us the innermost secret of who He is. We want that intimate disclosure without being serious about the relationship. As Ken Gire has observed, that's not much different from casual sex—wanting the pleasures of intimacy without the commitment. But Jesus is not indiscriminately intimate.[9]

So what will you choose for your life? You know what God is asking you to do, you know how God is asking you to live, you know what this is about, *and you know what it will take.* What's your decision going to be? Are you going to be quick to say, "Sign me up" but then ignore the cost? Will you just pay lip service to the whole deal and then bail at the first sign of sacrifice? Are you going to say, "Maybe later" and then walk away, thinking that there will be some time in the future when it's convenient for you to work God into your life? Are you going to say, "Yes, but . . ." and then fill in the blank with whatever it is you *don't* want to change, give up, do, or become?

Or are you going to follow Him?

Make no mistake: Only one of those responses will give you the life you really want to live. Because your spiritual life is not just another aspect of your existence, nicely situated alongside your financial life or vocational life. A spiritual life is simply another way of talking about life *itself*—every moment and every facet of it—from God's perspective.[10]

Several years ago, I spent a week in San Antonio, Texas. San Antonio is rich in American history, holding what is perhaps the most famous battleground in the West: the Alamo.

The Alamo was a Spanish mission. After Mexico won her independence from Spain, Texans wanted to be liberated from Mexico and join the United States. When they declared their independence, the Alamo went from a mission to a fortress, and Texans took their stand within her walls. The Mexican dictator, Santa Anna, marched toward the Alamo to crush the rebellion. Only 188 men were inside, but they included such legendary figures as Davy Crockett and Sam Bowie. Those men held off nearly four thousand Mexican troops for almost two weeks.

When you visit the Alamo, you can still see the holes made by bullets and cannon blasts. All 188 men were eventually killed, but their resistance gave Texas time to assemble an army that would eventually defeat Mexico and give Texas her independence. The battle cry during that war was "Remember the Alamo!"

But there is a side to the story that many don't know. The men of the Alamo knew that they were fighting against the odds. Their leader, Colonel William Barret Travis, gathered them together and told them they had a choice. They could leave the fort while there was still time, or they could stay and meet certain death. Then Travis unsheathed his sword, drew a line on the ground, and said these words: "Those prepared to give their lives in freedom's cause, come over to me."

Without hesitation, every man except one—which is how we know the story—crossed the line. Colonel James Bowie, inventor of the Bowie knife, was ill with typhoid pneumonia and couldn't walk across the line, but he asked that his *bed* be carried over.

For every one of us there is a line drawn in the sand—the line of commitment. You can grow in your relationship with Christ, achieving increasing levels of intimacy with Him. You can experience life change, becoming a walking reflection of how God can impact the character and habits, lifestyle, and attitudes of a human being. You can make a difference with your life by giving your resources and putting your spiritual gifts into play. You can have the life you've *always wanted*—but not without the final ingredient: *commitment*.

You have to cross the line. Purpose it in your heart. Seal it with a vow. Decide to follow Jesus—no turning back. When you do, you will experience the greatest journey available to the human soul: the spiritual life.

1. What might it cost someone to follow Christ?

2. What are some of the benefits of following Christ?

3. How would you explain to someone the importance of making this commitment?

4. How would the phrase "the life you've always wanted" help you explain Christianity to someone?

5. "You have to cross the line. Purpose it in your heart. Seal it with a vow. Decide to follow Jesus—no turning back." See (page 203.) What holds you back from giving your life totally to Christ?

Notes

Chapter 1: The Search for the Spiritual

1. The book I sent Dee-Dee was one I wrote for spiritual seekers titled *A Search for the Spiritual: Exploring Real Christianity* (Grand Rapids: Baker, 1998). A number of books have been written *about* seekers, for Christians to read in regard to their seeking friends, but few have been designed and written explicitly for seekers to read for *themselves*. *A Search for the Spiritual* is uniquely written and designed for individual Christians and churches to put in the hands of seekers in order to help answer their questions and address their concerns.

2. Daniel J. Boorstin, *The Seekers: The Story of Man's Continuing Quest to Understand His World* (New York: Random House, 1998).

3. For example, note Wade Clark Roof's analysis of the spiritual quest of baby boomers in *A Generation of Seekers: The Spiritual Journeys of the Baby Boom Generation* (New York: HarperSanFrancisco, 1993), as well as Tom Beaudoin's similar examination of the spiritual journey of Generation X in *Virtual Faith: The Irreverent Spiritual Quest of Generation X* (San Francisco: Jossey-Bass, 1998).

4. Mitch Albom, *Tuesdays with Morrie: An Old Man, A Young Man, and Life's Greatest Lesson* (New York: Doubleday, 1997), 33.

5. Frederick Buechner, *Whistling in the Dark* (San Francisco: Harper and Row, 1988), 80.

6. Albom, *Tuesdays with Morrie*, 84.

7. Douglas Coupland, *Life After God* (New York: Pocket Books, 1994), 359.

8. Adapted from Gene Edward Veith, "The Dilbert Hoax," *World*, 6 December 1997, 21.

9. As quoted by Jules Lemaitre, *Jean Jacques Rousseau* (New York, 1907), 9.

10. Adapted from Bill Hybels, *Too Busy Not to Pray* (Downers Grove: InterVarsity, 1988), 54–55.

11. Philip Yancey, *The Jesus I Never Knew* (Grand Rapids: Zondervan, 1995), 132.

12. Adapted from Robert Frank, "As UPS Tries to Deliver More to Its Customers, Labor Problems Grow," *Wall Street Journal*, 23 May 1994, sec. A, p. 1.

13. Adapted from Chuck Swindoll, *Living Above the Level of Mediocrity* (Waco: Word, 1987).

14. Thomas Kelly, *A Testament of Devotion* (New York: Harper and Row, 1941), 19.

Chapter 2: Making a Change

1. The following has been adapted from the author's *A Search for the Spiritual*, 133–36.

2. This summary was adapted from Henrietta C. Mears, *What the Bible Is All About* (Ventura: Regal, 1983), 23. For more on the message of the Bible and the significance of Jesus' life, death, and resurrection, see the chapter titled "Jesus . . . So What?" in *A Search for the Spiritual*.

3. Adapted from Max Lucado, *And the Angels Were Silent* (Portland: Multnomah, 1992), 59.

4. C. S. Lewis, *The Screwtape Letters* (New York: MacMillan, 1982), 11.

5. Richard Foster, *The Celebration of Discipline* (San Francisco: Harper and Row, 1978), 1.

6. This analogy is a contemporized version from one given by Dallas Willard in *The Spirit of the Disciplines: Understanding How God Changes Lives* (San Francisco: Harper and Row, 1988).

7. Dallas Willard, *The Divine Conspiracy* (New York: HarperSanFrancisco, 1998), 273.

8. I am indebted to C. S. Lewis, particularly *The Screwtape Letters,* for this insight.

9. Ken Gire, *The Reflective Life* (Colorado Springs: Chariot Victor, 1998), 47.

Chapter 3: God's Manual for Spiritual Living

1. This adaptation of the story of Augustine has itself been adapted from the wonderful retelling by Charles Colson in *Loving God* (Grand Rapids: Zondervan, 1983), 45–53.

2. For further reading on the Bible's inspiration and whether the Bible can be trusted, see the author's chapter on the Bible in *A Search for the Spiritual,* 64–76.

3. Though there are many excellent translations, I am partial to the New International Version. An excellent paraphrase, which is less accurate because it is not a word-for-word translation but more of an attempt to capture the essential meaning of the text, is *The Message* by Eugene Peterson (NavPress).

4. Gire, *The Reflective Life,* 90.

5. Adapted from Gordon MacDonald, *The Life God Blesses* (Nashville: Thomas Nelson, 1994), 70.

6. For assistance on this, see the author's *A Search for the Spiritual.*

7. This analogy has been adapted from Lee Strobel, *Inside the Mind of Unchurched Harry and Mary* (Grand Rapids: Zondervan, 1995), 115–116.

8. On these and other questions, see Rick Warren's *Dynamic Bible Study Methods* (Wheaton: Victor, 1989).

Chapter 4: Talking to God

1. "What We Pray For," *The Charlotte Observer,* 28 March 1994, 11A.

2. "Why We Pray," *Life,* March 1994, 57.

3. E. Glenn Hinson, *The Reaffirmation of Prayer* (Nashville: Broadman, 1979), 16.

4. Brother Lawrence, *The Practice of the Presence of God,* trans. E. M. Blaiklock (Nashville: Thomas Nelson, 1982), 19.

5. Ibid., 38.

6. Tony Campolo, *You Can Make a Difference* (Waco: Word, 1984), 116.

7. Chuck Swindoll, *Strengthening Your Grip* (Waco: Word, 1982), 216.

8. C. S. Lewis, *The Screwtape Letters* (New York: Macmillan, 1982), 3.

9. Anne Lamott, *Traveling Mercies* (New York: Pantheon Books, 1999), 82.

10. Adapted from James Overstreet, "When E-mail Turns to J(unk)-Mail," *USA Today,* 26 September 1994, sec. B, p. 7.

11. This outline comes from Hybels, *Too Busy Not to Pray,* 74–83.

12. For more on the issue of pain and suffering, see the author's *A Search for the Spiritual,* 77–87; see also the two books by Philip Yancey on this subject, *Disappointment with God* (Grand Rapids: Zondervan, 1988) and *Where Is God When It Hurts?* (Grand Rapids: Zondervan, 1977).

13. The insights from the preceding two paragraphs are indebted to Hybels, *Too Busy Not to Pray,* 80.

14. Ibid., 85–95.

15. "Prayer of an unknown Confederate soldier," taken from G. Curtis Jones, *1000 Illustrations for Preaching and Teaching* (Nashville: Broadman, 1986), 298–99.

16. Hybels, *Too Busy Not to Pray,* 94.

17. Ibid., 11.

Chapter 5: Spending Time with God

1. I am not sure from where (or whom) I first began thinking of this scene from the life of Jesus as a model for our time with God, coupled with the impact it can have on our own. I am relatively confident that it is not wholly original with me.

2. This observation, as well as the dialogue from the movie *Nell,* is taken from Gire, *The Reflective Life,* 9–11. See also Mary Ann Evans, *Nell* (New York: Berkley Books, 1995), 243.

3. Kelly, *A Testament of Devotion,* 120.

4. On the two levels of life, see Kelly's *A Testament of Devotion,* 35–38.

5. As quoted by MacDonald, *The Life God Blesses,* 71.

6. Adapted from Lettie Cowman, *Springs in the Valley* (Grand Rapids: Zondervan, 1939), 196–97.

7. Ibid.; this quote was suggested to my thinking through Gordon MacDonald's *Restoring Your Spiritual Passion* (Nashville: Oliver Nelson, 1986), 26.

8. Foster, *Celebration of Discipline,* 15.

9. Dietrich Bonhoeffer, *Life Together: A Discussion of Christian Fellowship* (New York: Harper and Row, 1954), 79.

10. For more on how to read the Bible, see chapter 3.

11. On this, see Gire, *The Reflective Life,* 87–103.

12. Ibid., 89.

13. See chapter 4.

14. For a good discussion of these four movements, see Hybels, *Too Busy Not to Pray*, 49–60. Much within this section is indebted to Bill's insightful and thorough treatment of prayer.

15. Of particular challenge to me, as might be guessed by the language in this sentence, was the aforementioned book by Hybels, *Too Busy Not to Pray*.

16. On this approach, I am indebted to the little pamphlet *Seven Minutes a Day with God*, published by NavPress.

Chapter 6: The New Community

1. *Cheers* theme song. ASCAP.

2. The phrases "love and be loved," "know and be known," "serve and be served," and "celebrate and be celebrated" were suggested to my thinking by Bill Hybels, but it is my understanding that they were not original to him. Also, parts of this section have been adapted from the author's *Rethinking the Church* (Grand Rapids: Baker, 1997), particularly the chapter titled "Rethinking Community."

3. Quoted in Philip Yancey, *What's So Amazing About Grace?* (Grand Rapids: Zondervan, 1997), 175.

4. Adapted from Ken Blanchard, *We Are the Beloved: A Spiritual Journey* (Grand Rapids: Zondervan, 1994), 19–20.

5. Bill Wolfe, "Church Meeting Ends in Fray, Beleaguered Pastor Resigns Amid Turmoil," *The Courier-Journal*, 10 December 1990, 1A.

6. For a full description of the church as the new community and how church might be "rethought" in light of some of the concerns mentioned, see the author's *Rethinking the Church*.

7. Henry Cloud, *Changes That Heal* (New York: Harper Paperbacks, 1995), 55.

8. Adapted from John R.W. Stott, *Christian Basics* (Grand Rapids: Baker, 1991), 128.

9. Charles Colson, *The Body* (Dallas: Word, 1992), 131.

10. This story has been adapted from an address given by Henry Cloud at Willow Creek Community Church. See also his book, *Safe People* (Grand Rapids: Zondervan, 1995).

11. Bonhoeffer, *Life Together: A Discussion of Christian Fellowship*, 19.

12. Lamott, *Traveling Mercies*, 55.

13. Adapted from Lynne and Bill Hybels, *Rediscovering Church: The Story and Vision of Willow Creek Community Church* (Grand Rapids: Zondervan, 1995), 159.

14. Adapted from John Maxwell, *The Winning Attitude* (San Bernardino, Calif.: Here's Life, 1984), 76.

15. Ibid.

16. MacDonald, *Restoring Your Spiritual Passion*, 71–91. MacDonald has a fifth category, sandwiched between VIPs and VNPs: the VTPs, or "very trainable people" whom we are able to invest in.

17. Much of my thinking on mentoring is owed to one of my mentors, Paul Stanley, and his book *Connecting* (Colorado Springs: NavPress, 1992).

18. Cloud, *Safe People*, 62.

Chapter 7: How to Worship

1. As quoted by Cathy Lynn Grossman, "Holy Moses, superhero," *USA Today*, 16 December 1998, sec. D, p. 2.

2. Foster, *Celebration of Discipline*, 148.

3. Adapted from Tony Campolo, *Who Switched the Price Tags?* (Waco: Word, 1986), 150.

4. See Romans 6:1–11.

5. See Matthew 3:16, which references Jesus "coming up out" of the water.

6. See "Baptism, Wash" by G. R. Beasley-Murray in *The New International Dictionary of New Testament Theology*, ed. Colin Brown (Grand Rapids: Zondervan, 1986), 1:143–61.

7. From *Macbeth*, act 5, scene 5.

8. For background information on Christian baptism, see G. R. Beasley-Murray, *Baptism in the New Testament* (Grand Rapids: Eerdmans, 1962); Oscar Cullman, *Baptism in the New Testament* (Philadelphia: Westminster Press, 1950); along with the excellent chapter on baptism found in Ralph Martin's *The Worship of God* (Grand Rapids: Eerdmans, 1982), 124–44.

9. For background information on the Lord's Supper, see C. K. Barrett, *Church, Ministry, and Sacraments in the New Testament* (Grand Rapids: Eerdmans, 1985); Markus Barth, *Rediscovering the Lord's Supper* (Atlanta: John Knox, 1988); along with the excellent overview given by Ralph Martin in *The Worship of God*, 145–70.

Chapter 8: Becoming a Player

1. Adapted from Charles Swindoll, *Improving Your Serve* (Waco: Word, 1981), 34.

2. Ibid., 43–44.

3. Thomas Merton, *New Seeds of Contemplation* (New York: New Directions Books, 1961), 29.

4. Ibid., 30.

5. *Webster's New World Dictionary*, 2nd college ed. (New York: Simon and Schuster, 1982).

6. Stephen Pile, *The Incomplete Book of Failures*.

7. From the Springfield, Oregon, Public Schools Newsletter, as quoted in Charles Swindoll, *Growing Strong in the Seasons of Life* (Portland: Multnomah, 1983), 312.

8. There are a number of good resources available on the subject of spiritual gifts, such as Bruce Bugbee's *What You Do Best in the Body of Christ* (Grand Rapids: Zondervan, 1995).

9. Acknowledgements to Ken Gire in his *Windows for the Soul* (Grand Rapids: Zondervan, 1996), 48, for first suggesting this analogy to my thinking.

10. One of the most popular spiritual gift courses, one I would personally recommend, is Networking, available through Zondervan and the Willow Creek Association. This course not only helps people discover their spiritual gifts, but ties it in with their passions and personality types. It is very useful in the life of the church.

11. To go further with this, see Gordon MacDonald's *Ordering Your Private World* (Chicago: Moody, 1984); Charles Hummel's *Freedom from Tyranny of the Urgent* (Downers Grove: InterVarsity, 1997); and Richard Swenson's *Margin* (Colorado Springs: NavPress, 1992).

12. Adapted from Campolo, *Who Switched the Price Tags?* 117–18.

Chapter 9: Positioning Your Heart

1. I'm not sure who owns this joke. I once heard it attributed to Bob Hope. Regardless, it is far from original with me.

2. Quoted from John Bisagno.

3. On this, see Ron Blue, *Master Your Money* (Nashville: Thomas Nelson, 1991), 17–24.

4. Blue, *Master Your Money,* 55–68.

5. This illustration was taken from Jerry and Ramona Tuma, *Smart Money* (Sisters, Ore.: Multnomah, 1994), 170–71.

6. Adapted from Blue, *Master Your Money*, 42.

7. Adapted from Swindoll, *Improving Your Serve*, 52–53.

Chapter 10: Impacting a Destiny

1. The speaker was Bill Hybels, used as part of an introduction to a series he gave on evangelism at Willow Creek Community Church in South Barrington, Illinois. See also the book Bill wrote with Mark Mittelberg, *Becoming a Contagious Christian* (Grand Rapids: Zondervan, 1994).

2. "Thank You" by Ray Boltz (ASCAP).

3. Adapted from the telling of the story by Les Parrot at the WCA Church Leadership Conference, August 1998.

4. I have portrayed the communication event of evangelism in the lowest possible key, with a very low "content" quotient. You should become as knowledgeable as possible, however, in regard to talking about your faith. Your church has, no doubt, training opportunities that you should take advantage of. If not, I would recommend the *Becoming a Contagious Christian* course (Zondervan/Willow Creek Resources).

5. Adapted from Campolo, *You Can Make a Difference*, 48–49.

6. Adapted from Gire, *The Reflective Life*, 172–74.

7. Hybels and Mittelberg, *Becoming a Contagious Christian*, 194–95.

Chapter 11: The Committed Life

1. Source unknown.

2. Adapted from Campolo, *You Can Make a Difference*, 11–13.

3. Adapted from Bill Barnhart, "Market Report: In the Heat of Battle, Traders Rule," *Chicago Tribune*, 25 April 1994, sec. 4, p. 1.

4. Swindoll, *Improving Your Serve*, 29. I adapted this from that quotation of Wilbur Rees, "$3 Worth of God."

5. This illustration was given by Os Guinness during an address heard by the author.

6. Adapted from Craig Brian Larson, ed., *Illustrations for Preaching and Teaching from Leadership Journal* (Grand Rapids: Baker, 1993), 215.

7. Adapted from Mrs. Howard Taylor, *Borden of Yale '09: The Life That Counts* (China Inland Mission, 1927).

8. This phrasing is borrowed, with slight modification, from the title of Eugene Peterson's *A Long Obedience in the Same Direction* (Downers Grove: InterVarsity Press, 1980).

9. Gire, *Windows of the Soul*, 174.

10. John Ortberg, *The Life You've Always Wanted* (Grand Rapids: Zondervan, 1997), 17.

Suggested Reading

I highly recommend the following books for the ongoing development and growth of your spiritual life. I have purposely chosen books written on a popular level by contemporary authors which are available through any Christian bookstore.

If someone in my church asked me for a handful of titles that have been particularly strategic in my own spiritual life and that I think would be strategic in their own, this is the list they would receive:

Blackaby, Henry. *Experiencing God.* Nashville: Broadman and Holman, 1994.

Colson, Charles. *Loving God.* Grand Rapids: Zondervan, 1983.

Crabb, Larry. *Inside Out.* Colorado Springs: NavPress, 1988.

Foster, Richard. *The Celebration of Discipline.* San Francisco: Harper and Row, 1978.

Gire, Ken. *Moments with the Savior.* Grand Rapids: Zondervan, 1998.

Gire, Ken. *The Reflective Life.* Colorado Springs: Chariot Victor, 1998.

Hybels, Bill. *Honest to God: Becoming an Authentic Christian.* Grand Rapids: Zondervan, 1990.

Keller, Phillip. *A Shepherd Looks at Psalm 23.* Grand Rapids: Zondervan, 1970.

Kelly, Thomas R. *A Testament of Devotion.* New York: Harper and Row, 1941.

Kempis, Thomas á. *The Imitation of Christ.* New York: Sheed and Ward, 1950.

Lawrence, Brother. *The Practice of the Presence of God.* Translated by E. M. Blaiklock. Nashville: Thomas Nelson, 1981.

Lewis, C. S. *The Screwtape Letters.* New York: MacMillan, 1982.

MacDonald, Gordon. *Ordering Your Private World.* Chicago: Moody, 1984.

MacDonald, Gordon. *Restoring Your Spiritual Passion.* Nashville: Oliver Nelson, 1986.

Mears, Henrietta. *What the Bible Is All About.* Ventura: Regal, 1983.

Ortberg, John. *The Life You've Always Wanted.* Grand Rapids: Zondervan, 1997.

Packer, J. I. *Knowing God.* Downers Grove: InterVarsity, 1973.

Sproul, R. C. *Knowing Scripture.* Downers Grove: InterVarsity, 1977.

Stott, John R. W. *Basic Christianity.* Grand Rapids: Eerdmans, 1971.

Swindoll, Charles. *Improving Your Serve.* Waco: Word, 1981.

White, John. *The Fight.* Downers Grove: InterVarsity, 1976.

Willard, Dallas. *The Spirit of the Disciplines.* New York: HarperCollins, 1988.

Yancey, Philip. *What's So Amazing About Grace?* Grand Rapids: Zondervan, 1997.

Yancey, Philip. *The Jesus I Never Knew.* Grand Rapids: Zondervan, 1996.

About the Author

JAMES EMERY WHITE is the founding and senior pastor of Mecklenburg Community Church in Charlotte, North Carolina. Started in a Hilton hotel in October 1992, Mecklenburg is often cited as one of the fastest-growing church starts in the United States, experiencing more than 80 percent of its growth from the unchurched. This has generated widespread attention from the media, including *CBS Evening News* and *USA Today*.

Mecklenburg adheres to a unique philosophy of ministry. The weekend services use drama, multimedia, contemporary music, and practical messages to present the timeless truths of Scripture at an introductory level that can be easily understood by unchurched people. The low-key evangelistic environment of the weekend services stands in marked contrast to the worshipful atmosphere of the midweek service, when believers gather together for worship, communion, and in-depth Bible teaching. An extensive network of small groups, meeting in homes throughout the community, fosters relationships and spiritual growth. Mecklenburg recently completed the first phase of an eighty-two-acre campus.

Dr. White holds a B.S. degree in public relations and business from Appalachian State University and M.Div. and Ph.D. degrees from The Southern Baptist Theological Seminary, where he was awarded a Garrett Teaching Fellowship in both New Testament and Theology. He has also done advanced graduate study at Vanderbilt University in American religious history. He has served as a visiting professor at such institutions as The Southern Baptist Theological Seminary and the Moscow Theological Institute. He is currently serving as the adjunct professor of Christian Theology at Gordon-Conwell Theological Seminary and on the President's Advisory Council of Union University.

An international speaker and consultant, Dr. White is the author of *Rethinking the Church* and *A Search for the Spiritual*. He also served as the consulting editor and contributing author to *The Holman Bible Handbook* and *The Holman Concise Bible Commentary*, as well as a contributing author to many other books.

Though his family's roots have been tied to North Carolina for generations, he was born in Chicago and then lived in California, Utah, and Washington. His family returned to North Carolina during his teen years. A basketball fan, Jim follows the Charlotte Hornets with great enthusiasm. Jim and his wife, Susan, live in Charlotte, where they homeschool their four children: Rebecca, Rachel, Jonathan, and Zachary.